Boffin's Journey:
A Cat Tale for Readers Of All Ages

by
Bea Nergaard

Proctor Publications, LLC • USA

Published in the USA by
Proctor Publications, LLC
PO Box 2498
Ann Arbor, Michigan 48106

Publisher's Cataloging in Publication
(Provided by Quality Books, Inc.)

Nergaard, Bea
    Boffin's Journey / Bea Nergaard. -- 1st ed.
    p. cm.
    SUMMARY: An alley cat named Dirty Socks is adopted
and renamed Boffin by a kind woman with a large family
of cats, but it's not easy for him to learn how to behave
in his new social environment.
    LCCN: 98-68154
    ISBN: 1-882792-72-6

    1. Cats--Juvenile fiction. 2. Socialization--Juvenile
fiction. 3. Etiquette--Juvenile fiction. I. Title.

PZ7.N437747Bo 1998   [Fic]
                             QB198-1509

Dedicated

to

Stree Shakti, Kali, and Kathmandu

and

to all the cats I've ever known

Acknowledgments

I want to say thanks to:

Patricia O'Dowd who invited me to sit in on her creative writing class which prompted me to pursue an old dream, and to Scoop Proctor for wanting to publish the book;

Charles Baxter, Betty Bell, Alvia Golden, Jane Johnson, Russell Kildal, Mary Oliver, Beverly Phillips, Karl Pohrt, Tom Pohrt, Jocelyn and Valerie Sullivan-Ross, and Peg Smith-Venturi for their various acts of encouragement;

Ellen Cantarow, Annette Martin, and Ruth Petrie for their critiques of earlier versions;

the late Harald Bakkan and Doris Corbett. Harald read and critiqued the first draft; Doris was the enthusiastic and optimistic supporter that every writer needs. I am sorry that they are not here to celebrate its publication;

and lastly, I must thank Martha Vicinus who read and critiqued each draft, was unfailingly patient and encouraging, yet realistic. Without you, Martha, Boffin and his friends might be in the trash bin.

"I'm just an old alley cat, I am,
I'm just an old alley cat, I am,
that's whoo I am, ooh that's whooo I am,
I'm just an old alley cat."

Boffin's Journey

Chapter One

In the dark alley behind *Le Chat Noir* restaurant, a garbage can crashed to the ground followed by the snarls of two
toms. Their fangs glinted in the dim light. One crouched in the
shadows near the fence; the other's white markings against his
black suit made him more clearly visible. As they stepped cautiously, waiting for their chance to pounce, a third figure crept
silently along the top of the fence and then dropped down behind the shadowy cat. He sank his teeth into the cat's hind leg. A
scream ripped through the air. Without a backward look, the cat
tore away into the darkness.

Dirty Socks attacked a flea biting his white knee-socked
hind leg, "Scruff, glad you happened by."

"Yeah, we gotta keep Shadder in his place." Scruff yawned,
"But I'm dead beat, gotta find a place to sleep."

As Dirty Socks watched his friend pad away he hummed,
*"I'm just an old alley cat, I am, I'm just an old alley cat, I am,
that's whooo I am, oooh that's whooo I am, I'm just an old alley
cat."* He left the alley and started down the street. His stomach
rumbled, his ears felt hot. "Sure am hungry." Just before dawn,

he entered a house-lined street where he'd seen sleek fat cats peering out of the windows. As he sniffed the shrubs, he bumped into an old grey and white fellow stumbling along, half-asleep.

"You were in my way!" the cat yawned, his eyes crossed.

"Who are you?" Dirty Socks snarled, the hair on his neck rising. The cat took no notice. "Well, I'm starved."

Grey and White's eyes uncrossed and focused on Dirty Socks. "Follow me to The Room, there's lots to eat there."

Dirty Socks looked puzzled.

"My home. The Woman feeds us," he said, yawning hugely. "My name's Ten Lives, what's yours?" Without waiting for an answer, he turned and padded across the street and into a park.

Dirty Socks stared after him. "Move your feet," his inner voice scolded. "I don't know him," Dirty Socks protested. "Take a chance," the voice urged. "Got nothin' to lose," he mumbled as he started after Ten Lives.

The Room was a small cottage. The roof swept down over a cement patio on which stood a couple of chairs, a rocker, a couch, and a table piled high with dishes, pots, clothes, newspapers and books. Ten Lives crumpled into a ball in one corner of the couch and was soon snoring.

Dirty Socks looked around. Nothing to eat. Nothing stirred. Beyond the clearing around The Room, shrubs, rocks and trees emerged in the gray morning light.

He trotted down a path through the trees. Blue flowers carpeted the ground. "Pieces of the sky have fell down 'round my feet," he sang merrily off-key. A gentle slope slipped into a brook where the sun, peeping through the trees, dropped diamonds on the water. But no fish.

Dirty Socks watched light begin to chase the shadows in a dark wood which opened into a small meadow where birds were singing high overhead and that set his tail swishing and his teeth chattering. Suddenly a squirrel dashed out of the woods. It stopped abruptly to stare at him. Dirty Socks' whiskers twitched. The squirrel darted to a big maple. He raced after it. The squirrel scurried along a limb, paused, flicked its bushy tail and leapt to another tree. Dirty Socks raced after him, but the limb bent sharply and down he fell, crashing through a mossy surface. He landed with a thump in a black hole. Before he could shake the dirt, moss and leaves from his face, a dark form rushed past him toward an opening through which light was stealing. Dirty Socks followed. Before him stood a brown cat, her gold eyes round with annoyance. "You have broken the roof of my abode."

Dirty Socks stared at her. "I was chasin' a squirrel." His eyes dropped, his toes wiggled, he blinked at the light streaming through the hole he'd made in the big barrel overgrown with moss and grass. Out of the corner of his eye, he noted the curve of her dark nose, the tail curled around her small chocolate body, her chin held high. "Didn't mean to."

She snorted scornfully, "Were you going to devour the squirrel?"

"I'm sure hungry." he admitted. She rose, stretched, and started down the path. "Hey, who're you?"

She turned. "Are you addressing me? Rather, who are you?"

"Uh...oh...you see, Ten Lies..."

"Ah, Ten Lives would have invitationed you here. But his name is Ten Lives, not Lies." She padded away, chuckling, "But I expect he does."

Dirty Socks trailed behind the brown cat, then stopped at the edge of the woods. A calico cat sat washing her side, a ginger paced back and forth, and Ten Lives still snored on the couch. Were there a dozen cats? Hundreds perhaps? But he wasn't very good at numbers.

"I don't believe I've seen you around here before."

Dirty Socks started. "N..n..no." Where was the body that belonged to the voice? In the shrubs? On the path? He could see no one.

"Don't worry," the voice sighed, "we'll meet sometime."

Dirty Socks turned back to The Room. He didn't dare move into the open so he climbed the tree behind The Room, jumped to the roof, and bent over the edge. A woman appeared on the patio with a tray of colored bowls full of food. Placing them in a half-circle, she called, "Okay, Marmeduke, here Calico Cat, you're back, Ten Lives, good morning, Merlinda." Everyone raced across the yard. Dirty Socks' stomach rumbled. He stretched forward, then still further. Suddenly, he lost his balance and dropped right into the ginger's bowl. He snarled, the calico cat screamed and everyone scattered. The Woman stared in surprise. "Poor fellow," she cried softly, "your ribs are showing. When did you last eat?"

Dirty Socks stared back. She didn't touch him. No sudden movements. A soothing voice. He sat down, gave his side a quick lick, and glanced back at her. Rising, he stretched, walked up and rubbed himself against her. Her fingers touched his head, scratched him between the ears. That felt like more. A purr quivered his sides. More scratching. The purr steadied into an idle. "Such fine long whiskers!" Wasn't she going to feed him? "Boffin," she said softly, "that's what I'll call you." He twisted around her legs. Boffin? "Come along, you'll stay inside, Boffin. The others will have to get to know you before you can dine with them, especially Marmeduke and Calico Cat."

The Woman set some water and a large bowl of fish before him. As he gulped the last morsel, she said, "You'll sleep here tonight." Stuffed to his ear tufts, he staggered to a bed in the corner where he gave his whiskers and toes a cursory lick. Should he leave now? But the pillow was very soft. The Woman had called him Boffin. Being named must mean that he'd been invited to live here. And that grey and white fellow, Ten Lies, his new friend, wouldn't he be disappointed if he left? "Maybe I've been adopted," he murmured sleepily. Perhaps not quite yet by the cat clan, but thinking made him very tired. Dirty Socks...no, Boffin closed his eyes. He would decide what to do later.

Chapter Two

Boffin was hardly awake when he was plunged into a tub of soapy water. He struggled to escape, but The Woman gripped him and scolded, "Boffin, what filthy socks!" When she let him go, he raced to the tall grass by the gate.

Boffin began to lick the water out of his fur. "I'll run away," he muttered, "but I can't go to the alley lookin' like this." Lick, lick, lick. "Then I'll have to scramble for my dinner again." He spread his toes. "I could stay here but that orange job Marm'duke and Cal'co Cat aren't friendly." He frowned. "'Course... that crazy tom's in the alley." Maybe he'd stay a few more days.

Ten Lives strolled through the gate, yawning widely. He looked around. "Who're you talking to?"

"Just me."

Ten Lives eyed him. "You look like a drowned rat."

Boffin glared back, but dropped his eyes quickly. His tail

was ratty-looking, he knew; in fact, he looked like he'd fallen into the river. Lick, lick, lick. The drying job was taking forever. He burped. He'd stuffed himself at breakfast, could he hold all of this water? He folded his paws; the sun could finish the drying job.

"Your chest is as white as mine."

The words floated into Boffin's musings. Ten Lives was studying him. Boffin glanced down, then sat up to get a better look at his chest, toe and ankle socks on his front feet, one knee sock on the back, blindingly white against the black fur. Of course his whiskers had always gleamed white because he licked them so much.

A cat walked up and sat down beside Ten Lives. White as sheets snapping in the wind. Grass-green eyes deep as a wooded pool.

Ten Lives turned to her. "I meant to go with you on your morning stroll, Merlinda."

Her nose touched Ten Lives'. "Yes, my dear, as always." She turned to Boffin. "How elegant you look in your black coat and white socks!"

Boffin wiggled his toes. What did 'elegant' mean? He glanced shyly at the two cats. "I... I reckon you're kind of good friends."

Merlinda lay down beside Ten Lives. "We both came here fourteen years ago." Her eyes half-closed.

Ten Lives gazed fondly at her. "Merlinda was here first, but we're the elders. I ran away from The People on The Farm because they left. I'd nearly starved to death when The Woman found me lying beside the highway."

"The Woman called him Ten Lives because she was sure

he'd already had nine when she found him!" Merlinda purred. "But his eyes showed promise."

"Merlinda was a terror climbing up trees after birds and tumbling from branch to branch," Ten Lives remembered. "And did she howl the day she fell into a tub of water!"

Merlinda rose stiffly. "Come for the last bit of my walk, Ten Lives." Turning to Boffin, she said, "Cleanliness is next to godliness, you know."

Boffin watched the two old cats pad down the path and disappear around the bend. What did she mean? Putting his chin on his paws, he gazed wistfully ahead. "I'm clean and fed, and I left the Shadow in the alley." Yet the ginger's snarling face and the calico cat's hunched figure flashed across his mind. If only he had a friend like Merlinda.

To cheer himself up in the alley, Boffin used to play a game that someone - his mother? - had taught him: when he was unhappy, he'd daydream a wish. He pretended that he was lying on a white cloud covered with bluebells and buttercups. Today a fluffy grey kitten came skipping along a sun ray, the light streaming through her long hair. Her head looked like a dandelion puff. She somersaulted right into his chest, bumped against him as softly as a feather, then curled up under his chin and fell asleep, her little pink nose tucked in his ear, snoring gently. Her fur tickled his nose. Suddenly a fly buzzed in his ear. He slapped at it and moved into the shade. "If only a grey kitten really would gallop into my life," he sighed.

By late afternoon the sun was burning hot. Boffin's stomach began rumbling. "Must be eatin' time!" He raced to the edge of the woods. The brown cat sat quietly near the patio. The patchwork job, Calico Cat, lay eyeing Marmeduke, the ginger tiger, who was pacing back and forth muttering, "Din, din, din, din..."

As The Woman appeared carrying the tray, Boffin dashed to the first bowl she put down. Calico Cat lunged and sank her teeth into his ear. A searing pain shot through him. Someone snarled behind him. Boffin whipped around. Marmeduke slashed out, scratching his white nose. The Woman snatched Boffin. He bit her. She dropped him and off he sped through the woods to the brook.

Quivering with fury, Boffin began to wash his wounds. If he'd had a chance, he'd have crunched Marmeduke, flattened Calico Cat. But he bit the Woman - who fed him. His stomach rumbled. Was she angry? Would she feed him?

Boffin stole through the woods. The Woman, rocking on the patio, quickly spotted him. "Boffin, come here." He approached cautiously, stopping to look around. Where was Calico Cat? Marmeduke? "Your dinner's waiting for you." She scratched him between the ears as he curled around her legs. "You have to eat from your own bowl." What did she mean? But he'd think about it tomorrow. Right now, he pigged out.

Chapter Three

Boffin's old friend Scruff used to sing, "Ohhh, life can be a dream, ta tum di dum bum..." And then he'd moaned, "Me hunger's ate holes in me stomach."

Remembering Scruff, Boffin quaked, "Ohhhhh, life can be a dream..." His voice trailed off. "I sound like a rusty fiddle." He blinked, and The Room floated back into his mind. For days he'd not had to scrounge in the garbage cans. He had a safe comfortable bed. Company...sort of. He glanced at the patio. Calico Cat and Marmeduke were sitting staring into space. They weren't snarling this morning. Were they sick?

"How about a game of chase?" Marmeduke said suddenly.

Boffin scratched his ear. Had he been asked to play?

Calico Cat rose. "Come on, Boffin, beat you to the brook!" She raced off, her tail strung out behind her. Marmeduke followed.

Boffin sped after them. Soon at Marmeduke's heels, Boffin floated through the air, his whiskers quivering with excitement. Calico Cat glanced over her shoulder at him just as she tore around some trees and shrubs. They plunged through thick grass before bursting into the open. The brook lay below. Boffin was suddenly at the edge of the steep bank. Too late to stop, he hurtled through the air, high above the green water moving darkly below him. The brook was wider here than where he'd spent hours looking for fish. And deeper. Down he fell, then plop! He hit the water and sank. He rose, gasping for air, then paddled furiously. He crept onto the shore, shook himself and looked around. No Calico Cat, no Marmeduke in sight. He licked the water out of his coat. Where were they? Was this another of their tricks? Had they really meant to drown him? He shuddered.

At dinner, Calico Cat and Marmeduke cried, "What happened to you, Boffin? Why did you stop the chase?"

Boffin studied Calico Cat's gooseberry eyes, brushed across Marmeduke's unswerving yellow ones. He looked down. His inner voice was silent. He began picking at his food, but no longer hungry, he turned and left.

Several mornings later Boffin woke after an unusually good night's sleep. He rose on his toe tips and stretched his back upward mightily; then lowering himself slowly, he looked around. Suddenly he dashed across the yard, leapt high into the air after a bee, then twisted gracefully before floating down. Without pausing, he sped across the yard, scrambled up the oak, then dropped to the ground. His eyes darted in every direction. He tore across the yard again, flipped heels over head, turned several somersaults, and landed in a heap at Calico Cat's and Marmeduke's feet. He rolled over on his back to gaze at the world upside down.

"The scruff bag's weird," Marmeduke snorted.

Calico Cat rolled her eyes. "Decidedly."

Boffin sat up. He sniffed the air. Bright sunshine and blue sky, no one was going to spoil this day for him. Rising, he strutted to his place in the dining circle, his tail strung straight up. "Ohhhhh, where's the grubby porridge," he hummed, "the porridgy grub?" What was porridge? The Woman served pebbles, sort of flavored.

After breakfast, Boffin lay down at the edge of the clearing. What should he do today? His tongue swung across his cheeks a couple of times. Washing wasn't quite a habit yet, but he practiced when he remembered. He sensed Marmeduke and Calico Cat near him but ignored them.

"Ahh-chew!" Calico Cat sneezed.

Boffin lifted his nose, sniffed the air.

"We...we wondered if..." Marmeduke began.

Calico Cat said, "Would you like to go see the strange thing living near us? It's a rare... ah.. thing."

Boffin ran his eyes over them. He studied the tree tops. He considered. Slowly he rose, stretched his front legs forward, raised his rear high as his long black tail curled into a question mark. He licked his side a couple of times. "Okay," he said at last, "where to?"

Boffin followed them to the third house down the street. Here they skirted the shrubs along the side to the back of the yard. Marmeduke looked at the building against the back fence. "It is in there."

Boffin stared at the building. "It?"

"The door will open soon and you'll be able to go in and look at It," Calico Cat whispered.

"What's It?"

"You'll see," Marmeduke said. "When a Person comes out,

the door will open and we have to run in."

Boffin frowned. "How do you know It's in there?"

"We were just passing this morning and we happened to catch a glimpse of It," Marmeduke said. "Just luck!"

Boffin was silent for a long time. "I saw an It once when I was with my friend Scruff. We were just wanderin' by a buildin' just like this one. We were lucky because we happened by just at the right time."

Calico Cat looked doubtful. "What did It look like?"

"Kind of scary, but you know. The buildin' It was in was just like this, that's where they hang out." Boffin's eyes never wavered as he looked from one to the other. "Can't describe It 'cause It ain't like anything you ever saw. You got to feel It before you'll be able to see It."

"It's probably not the same as this," Marmeduke said.

"Same hidin' place as this, big door, window on each side. Me and Scruff both went in."

Marmeduke's tail had sunk to the ground, but Boffin could see Calico Cat's curiosity scratching as she swished her tail back and forth. Suddenly the door began to move up. "Okay, go in fast," Boffin whispered. He stepped just inside the door behind a spade leaning against the wall. Marmeduke was on the other side while Calico Cat ducked behind a wheel barrow at the far end.

Soon a Person walked into the building and got into the car. When the motor started, Boffin slipped out and waited behind a shrub. When the car was out, the door slid down. Marmeduke tore out just in time. Boffin moved to the driveway. "Mmm, Calico Cat must be locked in."

Marmeduke glared at Boffin. "You knew."

"Knew what?" Boffin asked. A squirrel was chirping overhead. Boffin's tail swished, but he ignored the bright eyes staring down. "Knew about It? So did you."

"She might be in there forever," Marmeduke groaned.

"Yep. She might even starve to death. That happened in the alley more than once." Boffin trailed behind Marmeduke. "Poor Cal'co Cat, I feel really bad." He'd not intended to get Calico Cat locked in. When would the garage door open? Boffin felt his insides jiggle like the jello he and Scruff had found behind *Le Chat Noir* once. He hadn't liked the taste of it.

Chapter Four

Calico Cat didn't return that day or the next. Around Marmeduke, Boffin hummed, "Ohhh-ah, life can be a dream, ti dum ti dum bum..." but inwardly his stomach churned and he wondered how hungry Calico Cat was, was she frightened, might she starve to death?

The third morning Calico Cat was missing, Boffin was late for breakfast. Only the brown cat and a grey tiger were still there. Boffin didn't really know them yet. The brown cat was picking dainty bites out of her bowl while the grey tiger munched noisily. Boffin stared at his empty bowl. "Where's my breakfast?

The brown cat looked up. "Marmeduke ate it."

Boffin's stomach felt even emptier. "Wha.. what're your names?"

"Kanpur. You broke the roof of my abode."

Boffin studied his socks. "Yeah, I sure didn't mean to." He glanced up. "Kanpur, what a funny name! Kind of fancy. What's the other one called?"

The grey tiger blurted out, "I told you our runways would

cross." Then she turned and hurried away.

Boffin stared as she strolled across the yard and climbed the oak. "The voice! I heard her the first mornin' I was here!" He turned to Kanpur excitedly. "Who's she? What's she called?"

"Amelia Airheart. I do not know her well. She is not conversational." Kanpur's tongue slid over her cheeks. She rose and walked toward the woods, but before she disappeared she called, "Do not think about your hunger."

Boffin started. Could Kanpur, like Merlinda, read his thoughts? His mind circled back to the other cat. Might she become his special friend?

He leapt over the gate into the street. The day was golden-blue, the sun warm on his back. Through the black slivers dividing the golden-green pools of his eyes, Boffin stared at nothing in particular. He sniffed the scent of the blossoms, the sweet new grass, the fragrance of fresh leaves. He remembered lazy days by the river, eating when he wanted, exploring... then suddenly Marmeduke and Calico Cat galloped into his mind. Again. They made his head ache. Marmeduke didn't attack him now, but Boffin didn't trust him. And Calico Cat was locked in the garage. She'd be hungrier than he was now. Maybe something had fallen on her, maybe she was lying on the floor, bleeding, not able to get up or call for help. Should he lead The Woman to the building she was in?

Just then, a butterfly drifted by. Boffin's whiskers twitched. A bird trilling high overhead set his tail swishing. Near the forsythia, its young leaves gleaming bright green, stood the cherry tree dropping petals from its blossoms. Should he try to catch them? But he felt rather lazy this morning. His eyes lit on a drop of sunlight - or was it melted butter? - wafting gently toward the curb. It landed - plunk! on the edge of the sidewalk. A fragrant, delicate petal. Something lying in the gutter caught Boffin's eye. A motionless heap. He yawned, stretched, sat down, and again his eye lighted on the heap. Slowly he rose, stretched his elastic body, and padded over. He sniffed. A cat? Maybe. Not like any he'd ever seen. Blood? It wasn't dead, Boffin had seen dead animals in the alley.

The Woman swung through the gate. "Boffin, you're going to the vet's for shots." She stopped. "What's this?" Boffin twisted around her legs. "It needs help, poor thing!" A paw twitched, a cheek rippled, a gold-flecked eye rolled. "Wait, Boffin, I'll get a box."

Vet White Coat pulled open Boffin's mouth, poked his body and stuck him with needles. Then she locked him in a cage for many boring hours. He thought so hard about how to escape that he fell asleep with his nose buried in his fur, his paw thrown over his eyes, dreaming about the dappled light on the sidewalk. He chased petals floating down, and was about to catch a mouse that flew like a robin when the cage door rattled. Vet White Coat was back. He yawned. The mousy robin probably would have flown away because he'd wakened with his mouth open.

Vet White Coat then fetched a tiny grey fur so thin that Boffin's eyes could feel her ribs. Gold flecks in green eyes. This was the heap. He spit at the creature and leapt to the floor, pacing back and forth, slashing his tail. "Boffin!" The Woman scolded. Vet White Coat said the little one would soon be tearing around. Boffin spit again. If a faint breeze didn't whip away this paper cut-out, the fur clan would soon put the urchin in her place.

Marmeduke quickly blamed Boffin for dragging home riff-raff. Amelia Airheart didn't seem to notice the mite. The two elders looked on silently while Kanpur murmured, "A little silver thing."

Just then, a familiar cry filled the air - Calico Cat! Everyone turned as she leapt from the top of the gate and raced to the patio, meowing loudly.

"Calico Cat!" The Woman cried, sweeping her into her arms. "I looked everywhere for you. You must be starved!"

She was, but she took time to spit at the tiny newcomer before she plunged into the fish and cream that The Woman set before her. "I got locked in a Garage," she told them between bites. "I crouched just inside the door, ready to rush out." Boffin watched her special meal disappear and wondered if he should get lost for a few days. "I was so bored that I slept most of the time," she sighed, now washing her suit. "No one to talk to, nothing to eat or do, it was awful!" Marmeduke moved beside her. Boffin purred so loudly that everyone glanced in his direction, but Calico Cat never looked at him.

In the excitement of Calico Cat's return, the kitten was forgotten. For days she only ate and slept as she regained her strength. The Woman mused, "Until I know what she's like, I'll call her `Cat'."

One afternoon Cat woke up, stretched mightily, and looked around. Suddenly she scrambled up the oak. Amelia Airheart nearly fell off the branch she was dreaming on. Cat climbed so high that her little silver nose was a mere speck. "So how're you going to get down, Smartie?" Marmeduke yelled. Cat started down cautiously, tumbling from bough to bough, until she fell on Kanpur who screamed shrilly before she realized she'd lost her dignity. Cat next pounced on Marmeduke. His hair shot up and he slashed the air. Cat raced off to play hockey with a ball she'd spotted. Boffin watched closely.

Ten Lives eyed her darting here and there. "I'm gettin' too old to race around." Yet a distant memory fluttered across his mind and set his whiskers twitching, his tail tip flicking, and when Cat slapped the ball in his direction, he batted it. Startled, he stared at his paw, at Cat, then back at his paw.

Cat started after a cricket, somersaulted into Calico Cat who was washing her toes, then careered sideways.

"The channels have opened," Kanpur said, "the energy is flowing."

"Maybe she drank some of The Woman's beer?" Calico Cat wondered aloud.

"That skinny piece of fur is well," Merlinda mused. Just then Ten Lives tore after Cat. "Careful Ten Lives," she gasped, "you're not as young as you'd like to be."

Boffin followed by Calico Cat and Marmeduke dashed out. Amelia Airheart, who'd hung so far over a bough that only her claws had kept her from falling down, forgot her shyness and flew down to join in the fun. Even Kanpur raced a few steps before stopping to ponder if a dignified cat should tear around. As Marmeduke met Boffin, he screamed, "Get out of here, you scruff bag!"

Suddenly the kitten collapsed. The others dropped in furry heaps. The sun threw a bright glow across the yard outlining Cat, who lay in the center of the group. Ten Lives lifted his head. "She has a halo!"

"She's beautiful!" Boffin breathed softly to himself. "I imagined her, she'll be my special friend!"

The Woman was on the patio. "Her little head's like a dandelion puff. I'll call her Dandelion. What do you think of that, Merlinda?" she called to the old cat who was strolling to her cushion under the apple tree.

"Dandelion," Merlinda murmured as she settled down. "Dandelion, what kind of a name is that?"

Every day Boffin gazed at her, repeating, "Dand'lion, she's so pretty!" and "Dand'lion, what a pretty name!" He'd wake and exclaim, "I dreamed about Dand'lion!" Sometimes, he'd wonder, "Is she my Merlinda?" Her pink bowl was set between his and Marmeduke's. Boffin didn't stop purring. Dandelion turned and touched her nose to his, but she did the same with Marmeduke.

One grey morning, a mist hung in the air. Boffin woke up aching. Two meals a day and a soft pillow had not erased the pains in his joints. At breakfast Marmeduke watched Boffin wolf down his food. "You eat like a pig."

Boffin stopped eating.

"I want Amelia Airheart's place," Dandelion said.

Merlinda looked up. "Whatever for?"

"Boffin gets food all over his whiskers, and that spoils my appetite, to see food dangling from them, or stuck to the white fur of his cheeks."

Boffin hung his head. All eyes were on him. He wanted to cry, to throw up, to disappear. He glanced at Marmeduke and mumbled, "Marm'duke eats like a chicken."

"He does, he really does!" Calico Cat cried. Since Marmeduke followed Dandelion everywhere, Calico Cat was often alone now. Yet she still didn't talk to Boffin.

Dandelion cried, "You have such fine long whiskers, Boffin, they're so beautiful when they're clean. And they glow so...so shimmerly, like sun rays dancing on a spider's web - when food isn't hanging on them."

But Boffin had lost his appetite. He left his half-eaten breakfast. "She's too young to know any better," he moaned to himself. But deep down, he hurt a lot.

Chapter Five

Boffin was lying in his favorite place under a shrub near the oak dreaming about Dandelion although he hadn't forgotten her remark about his poor eating habits. Of course she chattered to him just as she did to any ear that listened, chattered even when there wasn't one.

This morning Marmeduke was watching dirt fly from a hole The Woman was digging. "What's The Woman doing?"

"Dunno," yawned Calico Cat. She hated not knowing so she padded over to check the softness of the soil heaps around the hole.

A spadeful of dirt nearly hit Ten Lives who'd stumbled over in search of a sunny spot. "What's going on here?"

Another spadeful just missed Marmeduke. "Ten Lives, what's The Woman doing?"

"Digging a hole, seems to me," he mumbled, turning around and around as he prepared to lie down.

"But what's it for?" Marmeduke persisted.

"A hole can be used for many things," said Calico Cat.

"For instance... " Boffin sneezed. She glanced quickly over her shoulder.

Just then Dandelion dashed over, batting her ball. She whacked it into the hole as she skidded to a stop.

"Your ball went in the hole," Marmeduke said.

Calico Cat nodded. "Yes, you can bat balls into holes."

"Is it a well?" Dandelion asked, peering down.

Kanpur strolled over and stood on the edge of the group. "A hole is a hole, things are what they are."

Overhearing snatches of the conversation, Merlinda padded over, her curiosity prickly as a burr. "As the wise cat in the clan, I must know what's going on."

Finally The Woman stood up. "Curious cats, you'll like my surprise," she chuckled as she climbed out. She filled the hole with water. Then she placed rocks here and there and planted grass over the dirt hills.

At first the cat clan padded up to the pond, cautiously dipped their paws in, and quickly withdrew them when they discovered it really was water. But ripples spread mysteriously in ever wider circles, twinkling in the sun. Fascinating.

One morning the air was clearer than usual, the sky bluer, the sun brighter. Boffin lay dreaming. Would Dandelion ask him to go for a walk? Instead Calico Cat strolled over. She'd become friendlier. She didn't ask him to go fishing or to chase butterflies, but sometimes she'd say, "You're up, Boffin!" when he padded over for breakfast or "How did you know it's dinner time?" Boffin blinked lazily at Calico Cat. Should he ask her if she'd ever tried holding a bird in her mouth when she was yawning? Or if she liked... but she was staring at the water. Boffin lifted his head. A

golden thing glittered, slid through the water, disappeared. Marmeduke and Dandelion wandered over. "Aah...aah...choo!" They all looked up. Amelia Airheart stared down from a branch that hung over the pond.

"Can you see it better from there?" Dandelion called.

"How do I know if I haven't seen it from the ground?" Amelia Airheart sniffed.

"Come down and tell us what those things in the pond are," Marmeduke shouted.

"If I knew, I could tell you from here," she retorted.

Calico Cat's eyes followed to the moving objects. "She'll only come down if her curiosity itches."

Kanpur padded up beside Boffin and gazed thoughtfully at the shimmer tracing golden threads through the water. "I wonder, has a piece of the sun fallen in... no, more than one, there are two, no three!"

Boffin leapt up. "Pieces of the sun fell in the water!" The message traveled across the yard like a prairie fire.

"Three pieces!" Calico Cat cried. Her paw hovered above the surface. "If it's the sun, the water'll be..."

"Hot! Hot! Boiling hot!" Marmeduke yelled.

Ten Lives sat up. "Just so, just so!"

Dandelion, quivering with excitement, leapt from rock to rock and nearly fell into the pond.

"Dandelion!" Marmeduke screamed. "Be careful! Don't fall in, you'll get boiled alive!"

"Just so, just so!" Ten Lives paced back and forth. "I haven't been so nervous since the day I lost one of my lives following Amelia Airheart up the oak."

A piece slid past. Calico Cat's paw flashed in and out. Stunned, she stared at her paw dripping water.

"Did you burn yourself?" gasped Marmeduke.

Dandelion rushed over. The pads seemed to swell before Calico Cat's eyes. Had she touched a piece of the sun? Was the paw turning bright red? But no pain, no redness, no swelling. "I...I don't know," she stammered.

Marmeduke shrieked, "You must know if you've burned yourself!"

Suddenly Amelia Airheart tumbled off her branch, her legs and tail flailing about, her eyes immense. Boffin stared as the falling figure hit the water and spattered drops that sent everyone scurrying. She sank from sight. Boffin leaped in and began paddling through the spreading rings, but before he reached Amelia Airheart, her head popped up. She splashed to the shore, crept past the astonished group and streaked up the oak tree. She'd disappeared in the leaves before Boffin was back on shore, shaking himself and sprinkling water everywhere.

"Problem is once you start falling down," Ten Lives rumbled, "you can't just change your mind and go back up."

Marmeduke snorted, "Stupid alley cat thought he could save Amelia Airheart!"

"Goldfish, how beautiful they are!" Merlinda's green eyes followed the flashing forms.

"That's so, that's so," Ten Lives rumbled.

Boffin's eyes widened. "Gold fish? Are they buttered?"

"Was the water hot, Boffin?" Dandelion whispered.

"You were so brave, Boffin!" Calico Cat exclaimed.

Boffin studied his blinding white ankle sock and toe sock. Without looking up, he slipped away along the path to the brook with Calico Cat's words ringing in his ears, Dandelion's face flashing across his mind. Had he been brave? He hated water.

The shadows along the banks danced silently to the trickling water in the fading light. Boffin felt warm inside. Soon the sun touched the tree tops. It must be dinner time. Boffin raced back to The Room. Eight bowls sat on the patio, shining, empty. His stomach growled. His tail sank to the ground. A shiver suddenly ran up his spine. He sensed someone near him. Had the Shadow followed him here? Slowly, he turned. But it was Marmeduke behind him, carefully grooming himself. He looked up. "Hungry?" he sneered.

Chapter Six

Although Boffin was now sometimes greeted with "Mornin', Boffin!" - "Let's go play by the stream, Boffin!" - Marmeduke's "You still here?" kept him wary. But today Boffin returned to the patio humming, "Ooooh, life can be a dream, ta tum di tum bum..." He and Dandelion had spent the morning among the trees that stretched up forever. On the table was a cake with more candles on it than Boffin could count, perhaps even too many for Merlinda. "Why's the table set like that?"

"Ten Lives' birthday party," Marmeduke said.

Dandelion looked puzzled. "How is a birthday party?"

"You don't how a birthday party, you who a birthday party," Calico Cat purred importantly.

Boffin frowned. "What's `birthday'?"

Calico Cat stared at him. "Weren't you ever born?"

Boffin scratched his ear. "Can't say I remember."

"You need a brain for that!" Marmeduke groaned and stared glumly at his feet; he was trying to be kinder to Boffin because he clearly wasn't leaving.

"Few remember," Kanpur said dreamily.

"Birthdays are like Christmas!" Marmeduke shouted.

Dandelion eyed the cake. "Is that a birthday too?"

"Yes," Calico Cat said. "I don't remember whose."

Dandelion cried, "We all get presents then!"

Calico Cat said, "Today Ten Lives gets the presents, it's his birthday."

But what to give him? Something you like very much? Or something useful like soap or flea powder?

Boffin frowned. "A towel would come in handy. That dryin' job is awfully fillin', especially after eatin'."

"I'll get Ten Lives sardines!" Dandelion cried.

"Ten Lies don't like them," Boffin reminded her.

"Oh, but I love them," Dandelion said, "and he'll let me eat them and that'll make us both happy."

Boffin thought he must be missing something.

After staring moodily at an ant hill, Calico Cat finally said, "Let's get our own gifts. The party's at five, Boffin, don't be late!" And off she galloped.

By late afternoon, everyone except Dandelion was lying in a circle around Ten Lives. Suddenly a loud thump, followed by a clatter of pots and pans from the patio, startled them. Chasing a ball across the yard flew Dandelion, her little legs a blur. She somersaulted into the circle and landed in a furry heap at Ten Lives' nose. "Happy birthday, Ten Lives," Dandelion squealed, giving her coat a few quick licks. She looked around, dashed after the ball and called, "I ate the sardines I got for you, Ten Lives, so here's your present. You can play hockey with me. Has the birthday party begun?"

"Obviously," came a dry response from the circle.

Dandelion plopped down in front of Ten Lives with her chin on the ball between her paws. She fell asleep.

Ten Lives hrrrumphed loudly. He sneezed. He yawned.

Amelia Airheart stepped forward. Her grey tiger stripes had a vacuumed, brushed look. "Happy birthday, Ten Lives. My gift disappeared." She stopped to stare at a lady bug crawling over a blade of grass.

Marmeduke snorted, "Disappeared?"

Amelia Airheart glanced up shyly. "I gathered some nuts for hockey pucks and put them on the ground last night. But the squirrels stole them."

"Took them back, you mean," Marmeduke sneered.

"By that time it was too late to gather more."

Marmeduke interrupted, "Well, I have a mirror for you, Ten Lives." He gazed at himself, twitched his whiskers, rolled his eyes.

Dandelion rushed to Marmeduke. "Let me see my halo." He whisked the mirror past her face. "The Woman said I have a halo like a dandelion, where is it?"

"Ten Lives," Kanpur began, "I rescued some milk and ice cream for you, but how to bring them here!" She licked something that still clung to the corners of her mouth. "Of course it is the thought that counts."

"Well, well!" The sound came from deeper than ever in Ten Lives' throat. He looked touched.

"Yes, the thought's important," Calico Cat cried, "so I found some butterflies fluttering their orange and blue and yellow spotted black velvet wings!" Calico Cat rolled her eyes dreamily. "I'd have brought some back for you, Ten Lives, but I couldn't catch them. Then I remembered what you said when Dandelion first came here. `I'm too old to play,' you said, so I played for you, I knew it would make you happy!" Calico Cat jumped up and galloped to Ten Lives, licked him on each cheek, and wished him a happy birthday.

Merlinda now opened her eyes. "Happy birthday, Ten Lives, I'm giving you my soft cushion under the apple tree. Lie and look up at the apple blossoms in the spring, they're so lovely." She closed her eyes and drifted into what everyone called a cat nap except Kanpur who said it was the meditative state.

Ten Lives gazed fondly at Merlinda. "I can't take your cushion. No, no, the cushion's yours, you keep it."

Merlinda murmured, "Is that everyone?" Sitting with his head hanging practically in his socks was Boffin. "Boffin, you haven't given Ten Lives your gift yet!"

Boffin shrank into an even smaller heap. He knew he'd missed the point of this birthday party, and now he sat twisting a feather in his paws. He coughed. "I..." He glanced at Merlinda, then remembered that it was Ten Lives' birthday so he turned to the center of the circle where Ten Lives had risen and stood looking at him. "Er," Boffin began, "ah, I found this in the woods for you, Ten Lies." He took a few steps forward. He stepped on the feather. Then just as he threw it towards Ten Lives, a gust of wind whipped through the yard. The feather wafted above their heads, and

30

hung for a moment before it floated to the top of a pine tree where the needles caught it. There it waved, bright red against the blue sky.

"A cardinal's feather," Ten Lives rumbled softly. "Thank you, Boffin." Boffin, his eyes lowered, stumbled back to his place. But his tail, held high, waved as gently as the feather in the pine tree.

"Look at Boffin's chicken feather in the tree!" Marmeduke snorted.

Before Merlinda could scold him, The Woman called, "Ten Lives' birthday dinner's served!" They all streaked to the patio where they stopped abruptly and stared. On the table sat Ten Lives in his grey suit with white chest and cheeks, white socks and whiskers, and pink nose, gazing out of a red frame, an elegant gentle-cat frozen in time. "It's impossible!" Boffin gasped; Ten Lives was standing right beside him. Boffin turned back and forth from Ten Lives to the picture .

"A photograph of Ten Lives," Merlinda murmured.

Suddenly the air was filled with the songs of all the birds Boffin had ever heard in the forest. His teeth chattered, his whiskers twitched, his tail swished back and forth. "How... Where... What's..."

Dandelion, her eyes as big and round as the full moon, was pawing a black box. "Are the birds in here?"

"It's...it's magic!" Boffin gasped as he stepped backwards, right into Marmeduke's birthday dinner.

"Get your big clodhoppers out of my food!" Marmeduke yelled. Boffin sprang up and nearly landed in Dandelion's dish.

"No magic," Calico Cat purred. "The Woman caught the

sound in the woods in that black box. And try not to step in anyone else's bowl, Boffin." Her eyes twinkled as she watched him licking his toes.

"Is Ten Lives pressed into the pa-  per?" Dandelion whispered.

Ten Lives looked from himself to his image. "Was I?"

Calico Cat rubbed her head against him. "Ten Lives is still here. That's his double on the table."

When Boffin finally turned to the birthday dinner, he couldn't believe the meal - fish cakes heaped with whipped cream. "When's my birthday?" he wondered as he ate and ate and ate.

Chapter Seven

After the birthday dinner, Boffin lay beside Merlinda and Ten Lives near the pond. He licked his glossy black side, admired his chest, mustache, and cheeks now whiter than freshly fallen snow. His beautiful long whiskers glinted in the sun as he twitched his cheeks. He'd seen Calico Cat silently admire them and everyone told him how magnificent they were, everyone except Marmeduke, of course, and Amelia Airheart who was very shy, and Kanpur who didn't talk a lot, and Ten Lives who probably hadn't noticed, but Dandelion and Merlinda had told him. Of course his socks were still a problem. Dandelion would ask him loudly, "Why aren't your socks as white as Ten Lives'?" - much to Marmeduke's delighted disgust. And even though Merlinda reminded Boffin that "Eating time's eating time," he regularly forgot his stomach as he watched fish or birds or dreamed about the alley now wrapped in rose-gold memories. He'd felt so free there.

"Ah, we used to have this weird cat in the alley we called the Shadow. He was sort of like one."

Merlinda's eyes popped open. "A shadow? A cat isn't a shadow."

"I'm grey, but I'm no shadow," Ten Lives yawned. "Of course Dandelion's grey but she's only a kitten. And as for Amelia Airheart, I'm not sure she's pure cat."

Amelia Airheart, perched on a branch, stared at Marmeduke poking around the base of the oak, sniffing the earth, testing the softness of the moss, turning around and around, lying down, getting up, turning around and finally settling down. He licked his orange stripes until they shone wetly. Finally he turned his face to the sun and closed his eyes.

Amelia Airheart was interesting in an odd sort of way, Boffin decided, putting his chin on his paws. He'd barely begun to walk into a dream when a fly buzzed in his ear. His eyes popped open just as Amelia Airheart dropped from her branch, her legs, tail and head spread like six points of a star. Down she floated like a leaf, and landed, very nearly on top of Marmeduke. He sprang straight up and screamed at Amelia Airheart who was already climbing back up the trunk.

Merlinda scolded, "Marmeduke's going to shake his fur loose."

"Why does 'melia' Airheart live in the oak tree?"

"Dunno," Ten Lives muttered. "Calico Cat says she doesn't like peop...er, furs, I mean cats, but Merlinda says she's shy. I reckon she's part squirrel, but her tail's not very fluffy. Probably Dandelion's part squirrel."

"Dandelion must be a ground squirrel then, she doesn't live in trees," Merlinda purred thoughtfully.

Calico Cat padded up just as Marmeduke stumbled over.

Dropping to the ground, he grumbled, "Crazy cat, only odd-balls live in trees, she's a crazy odd-ball."

"Unless it's a bird," Calico Cat said.

"Why's she called 'melia Airheart?" Boffin asked.

"She has real talent the way she floats down..."

But Marmeduke interrupted Calico Cat. "The rag bag's here!" Merlinda's stern look cut Marmeduke off.

Ten Lives yawned. "We all have some special talent."

"What's yours, Ten Lies?" Boffin asked, but only a snore answered.

Calico Cat sighed. "Poor Ten Lives often falls asleep on his feet."

"That's because Ten Lives and Merlinda are old," Marmeduke muttered. "Boffin wouldn't have noticed."

"Ancient," Calico Cat sighed. "They're at least twelve or fourteen, maybe even seventeen."

Boffin scratched his ear. "What's Merlinda's talent?"

"Merlinda!" Calico Cat exclaimed. "Merlinda's the wise cat of the clan!"

"How do you know?" Boffin asked.

"That's what I say," Marmeduke snapped.

"It's obvious," Ten Lives sighed, awake again. "When The Woman found Merlinda, she knew right away that she was in the presence of... uh... someone unusual."

"I think it's in her eyes," Calico Cat said hesitantly.

"Just so, just so," Ten Lives agreed. "She knows everything that's happening even when she's sleeping."

"The first day she was here Kanpur saw that Merlinda knows who walks up to her even when her eyes are closed.

That's why she's called Merlinda." Boffin looked puzzled so Calico Cat continued. "Of course growing up in the alley, you wouldn't know about Merlin. He was a wise old... was he a person or a fur face, er...one of us, Ten Lives?"

Marmeduke said quickly, "One of us, if he was wise."

"I suppose he was one of us. He was very, very wise, so wise that he had a white beard, like your chin-fur, Boffin, but long. Perhaps yours will grow, if you live long enough." Calico Cat looked doubtful.

"Will I get wise then too?" asked Boffin.

Marmeduke snorted. Ten Lives looked uncertain. Calico Cat studied Boffin for a moment, then said, "Wisdom is a strange thing. You don't catch wisdom like you catch a mouse and you don't grow it like you do long whiskers." She stole a glance at her white, black and orange patches. "A coat of many colors may help. It's kind of like having smartness or dumbness or kindness or..."

"Nastiness!" Marmeduke snapped, glaring at Amelia Airheart.

"The Woman was going to name Merlinda `Merlin', but when she discovered that she's a she, she called her Merlinda instead. I think `Merlinda' is so pretty."

"She is, she is!" Ten Lives agreed eagerly.

"Did you know Merlin?" Boffin asked.

"No, he lived long ago," Calico Cat said, "even before Merlinda and Ten Lives were born." Everyone became quiet, trying to imagine a time before any of them had been around. Ten Lives began to nod.

Dandelion skipped over. "Is this a party?"

Marmeduke said, "The Woman found me wandering around in the park. She said she just loved orange tigers, and marvelled at the very remarkable rings on my tail." He eyed his tail stretched out behind him, flicking gently. "I know my stripes are rare. When I lived in the Catsel, other gingers around there had very pale stripes, not really stripes at all."

"Why did you leave the Catsel?" Dandelion asked.

"There was a fire one night. I got so scar...startled that I ran away and by the time I stopped for breath, I was lost. I was lucky I got out. But I had such a soft bed there, fresh liver and fish every day - nothing canned. A cross-eyed mean Siamese lived there too, but," and his eyes became dreamy, "life was so elegant. When The Woman found me, she said, 'You're real Marmelady!' But I'm a he, I couldn't be called that. Then she said, 'You act like a duke!' I could tell she meant I'm a rare breed. So she called me Marmeduke."

"What's a rare breed?" Calico Cat demanded.

"Why, my family, of course," Marmeduke snorted. "I come from a very distinct family."

Calico Cat frowned. "Kanpur says she comes from a distinguished ancestry. Is that the same thing?"

The soft light sifting through Dandelion's long grey fur drew a halo around her. "The Woman said my tail's a plume," she sighed, flicking its tip gently.

"You're so pretty, Dand'line," Boffin murmured.

Marmeduke moved beside her. "You're my best friend."

"She may be your only friend," Calico Cat sniffed.

Marmeduke continued loftily, "Some of us are handsome."

"Not me," Ten Lives yawned. "I've big feet and my ears stick out. The Woman thought I was the floor mop yesterday."

"You have other wonderful qualities, Ten Lives," Calico Cat said, but she couldn't remember what they were. Marmeduke looked at him; he hadn't noticed any.

Ten Lives sat up. "Kanpur's had a real airplane ride."

"Unlike Amelia Airheart who only pretends to fly,' Marmeduke sneered.

"Kanpur," Boffin said, "such a dark choc'late..."

"She's Indian, you know," Calico Cat whispered.

Boffin's eyes widened. "How do you know?"

"One knows," Calico Cat sighed.

"Can you tell I come from the alley?" Boffin asked.

"Of course! And I am clearly not from the streets." Marmeduke snorted, gazing into the distance.

Ten Lives' whiskers twitched. "The Woman found Kanpur by the railway station, that's why she's Indian."

"Kanpur's from India," Marmeduke explained.

"What's India?" Boffin asked.

"It's very far away and much bigger than The Room," Calico Cat said softly. "When the Woman was gone, her Person Friend who stayed here got food all over his face and that looked even worse than the crumbs on your whiskers, Boffin."

"A cow in the street nearly stepped on Kanpur," Ten Lives said.

"Yes, almost squished her with its foot," Marmeduke added. "The Woman grabbed her just in time. She got off the train by mistake. She didn't mean to stop there."

"The Woman, not the cow," Calico Cat explained.

"Kanpur was already there, of course," Marmeduke said.

Merlinda's eyes opened a crack. "Kanpur calls it destiny; it was meant to be."

"The Woman rushed into the street, grabbed Kanpur, and stuffed her in her purse," Calico Cat cried, "and she carried her home in the airplane, all the way to The Room from India, stuffed in her purse!"

"She was so glad to get out she purred and purred when she got to The Room," Marmeduke said.

"Why's she called Kanpur? We can all purr."

"That's where The Woman found her," Marmeduke said.

"Named in honor of us!" Calico Cat's round eyes shone.

It must be an alley then, Boffin decided.

Suddenly, a shriek ripped through the air. Amelia Airheart flew from the oak and streaked across the yard to the patio. In a flash, the others followed. Boffin glimpsed a dark figure disappearing into the woods. Amelia Airheart hid under the couch, her whiskers vibrating. "What's going on?" - "What happened?" - "Did you get murdered?" everyone shouted.

"It.. it.. something s..s..started to c..c..climb the oooak!" Amelia Airheart stammered from the corner.

"What tried to climb your tree?" Merlinda demanded. "Is this your imagination?"

"S..s..something...l..like a d..d..dark..."

"The Shadow," Boffin muttered.

Merlinda turned to Boffin. "You mentioned a shadow earlier, is this it?"

Boffin's eyes dropped to his toes.

Marmeduke glared at Boffin. "The alley cat's to blame. He dragged one of his kooky pals here. We'll all be murdered one of these nights. Flea-bitten scrap of worn-out fur, I won't have him near me. We're not safe with him here."

Boffin slipped to the far side of the apple tree to sleep. The cat clan, crowded under and on top of the couch, didn't want him near them, he knew.

Chapter Eight

The Shadow haunted The Room although no one saw
him. The cat clan hung around the patio during the day and slept
there at night. Day after day, Merlinda would stare out and mut-
ter, "There's something out there."

Boffin had never felt lonelier. Marmeduke snarled, "The
alley cat's to blame!" and the others would scream, "Stop that!" -
"Don't be so..." - "Leave us if you can't..." To Calico Cat, Boffin
could have been a fly on the wall. Dandelion sometimes forgot to
be angry with him as she'd cry, "Look, Boffin, there's a robin!"
But her friendliness was like bloom that goes to seed, scattered
by each day's breeze. Boffin dared speak to no one, not even Ten
Lives.

When the Shadow didn't return for many days, Amelia
Airheart climbed the oak again because she couldn't stand the
crowd. Kanpur, who thought the Shadow was either a figment of
the imagination or some harmless creature, returned to her hideout. Tired of the snapping, Merlinda returned to the apple tree

and strolled through the woods every morning with Ten Lives. They all lounged around the pond at mid-day, dipped their paws in the water, or chased butterflies. One day, as Boffin dreamed under his shrub, Calico Cat's voice roused him.

"Marmeduke claims he's a rare breed." Calico Cat was studying a bee crawling over a rose. She scratched her ear. "Kanpur's from distinguished ancestry, but I have the only coat of three colors." She paused. "The Woman says my relatives are in a shop downtown so my family must be the most distinct ancester breed." She looked up. "Who'll come with me to find my relatives?"

"Most cats have no idea who their relatives are." Every head lifted. Amelia Airheart had spoken.

"Every self-respecting cat ought to know who her mother is," Merlinda retorted from under the apple tree.

"Bet my mother was orange and my father was black," Calico Cat reflected, gazing dreamily at the bee.

"And where did you get the white splotches, from a rabbit?" Marmeduke charged, squinting in the grass.

Eyeing her orange, white and black patched figure, she sniffed, "I was born in the middle of summer."

Dandelion was admiring her reflection in the water. "Ten Lives and Boffin have white patches too, do you three have the same mom?"

Ten Lives mumbled, "No no, I reckon not."

Marmeduke said, "My dad was a big tiger, king of the cats. He had his pick of... well, my mom found him when he'd gotten his ear torn in a fight with this huge tom..."

"Kings don't lose fights," Boffin interrupted.

"He just got a torn ear, stupid," Marmeduke retorted.

"To bask in the reputation of ancestors is only reflected glory," Kanpur mused.

"What's Kanpur mean?" Marmeduke whispered to Dandelion.

"No one can steal my halo," she replied without taking her eyes off her image.

"We may all have royalty in our ancestral backgrounds," Kanpur said thoughtfully. "I may have been a queen."

"I was an only kitten," Marmeduke said. "I got the rings on my tail from my mom." He turned to gaze at the admired appendage stretched out behind him.

Ten Lives said gruffly, "My mom was grey striped like Amelia Airheart, but wonderful. She taught us to hunt because she said when we left her we might be served saucers of cream or have to root around in garbage cans."

"My ancestry is very ancient," Kanpur mused. "I am Burmese, you know."

"I thought you were Indian," Dandelion said.

"I was birthed in India," Kanpur sighed, "but my progenitors were Burmese. This deep brown comes from them."

"What's `progenitors'?" Marmeduke asked.

"Cousins, aunts and uncles and sisters and brothers," Calico Cat said loftily. "But it's hard to understand."

"My ancestry probably goes back further than anyone's."

"Because you're so old, Ten Lives?" Dandelion asked.

"Don't be rude," Merlinda scolded.

Kanpur objected, "India is much older than The Room."

"Someone must come with me to that shop where The

Woman says calico cats live," Calico Cat cried. "I must know where I come from. Otherwise how can I know who I am?"

Boffin was fascinated by Dandelion's changing face as she rippled the water with her paw. She stretched her neck to look at her tail but it hung too far back. He rose, stretched, sat down, and gave himself a couple of careless licks. "I'll go with you, Cal'co Cat. Where do we go?"

"Downtown. Near a small park, there's a tobacco store on the corner and I think a restaurant. Do you know where..."

Boffin's eyes brightened. "Ah, *Le Chat Noir*! The French restaurant! I've ate there a lot - poulet à la crème, poisson en beurre..." Past feasts drifted by, complete with their scents as his old buddies gathered around him - timid Mustard and battle-scarred Boxer, old Scruff in his worn dusty fur, nervous Rarebit... Boffin blinked. Marmeduke was glaring at him suspiciously, Ten Lives had sat up, Calico Cat stared at him, and Dandelion had moved beside him: was this the Boffin who got food all over his face? "Chicken cooked in cream and fish fried in butter," he yawned. "We even ate ice cream. Best leave at sundown, Cal'co Cat. And we'll go to the restaurant after we've seen your relatives."

Marmeduke snorted. "He'll get you lost."

Calico Cat eyed him. "Do you really know the way?"

"The tobacco shop's near *Le Chat Noir*, I've ate there many times, the smell's easy to find."

Dandelion's eyes grew wide. "What did you get to eat at the tobacco shop?"

"Rest now," Boffin told Calico Cat. "It's goin' to be a long night and we gotta be sharp." Voices drifted in and out of Boffin's sleep. While Ten Lives reviewed his past lives, Marmeduke announced to no one in particular, but of course to everyone, "At the Catsel we dined on..."

"Imagination creates ancestors," Kanpur mused. "If beggars or thieves turn up, will one claim them too? Better to study one's reflection in the pond."

"Boffin's a beggar," Marmeduke reminded everyone. "That's what an alley cat is, a beggar."

"For those who care about ancestors, that is the sort of thing they care about." Merlinda buried her nose in her fur.

When the sun sank below the horizon, Boffin rose. "Time to go, Cal'co Cat." The others watched them disappear down the street into the dusk, their tails high.

Calico Cat had to trot, sometimes gallop, to keep up to Boffin. "The Woman called me Calico Cat because that's what I am. Now don't you think I ought to know where I come from if I'm a calico cat?" she puffed. "The calico cats are in the shop that's called *Find It Here*. It's odd I didn't come from there, don't you think?" Boffin half-listened to the words spill out of Calico Cat's mouth as he watched for danger on the streets and in the parks and alleys.

"It's odd, because you know, or you probably don't, that none of the fur clan come from *Find It Here*. Calico cats must be special if they can be adopted from shops." She paused, then added, "Since I'm the only calico cat that didn't come from that shop, I must be even more special, in a different sort of way." She paused again. "I've long known that I am unusual. I hope it doesn't make you feel bad, but it probably does. At least I'd feel bad if I were ordinary and had to live with someone who is very unusual. Of course Marmeduke thinks he's an aristocat, but we know that means nothing, so it isn't hard to live with."

Boffin saw that the cars whizzing by, dogs barking, bright lights flashing, and shadowy figures milling around made Calico Cat jumpy. "Would you like to rest awhile?"

Calico Cat glanced nervously around. "I'm quite unused to this, Boffin, but let's go on. Tell me about your alley life. You seem so...so street-wise."

"Not all Persons like us," Boffin warned as they circled around a group of them. In a garbage-strewn alley he continued, "I fought a old ginger here. He lived on the streets all his life. He learned me a lot."

"Where is he now?" Calico Cat whispered.

"Dunno," Boffin said, his eyes darting from side to side, "he got ran over."

Calico Cat's eyes shone like dark pools. "Oh my! Oh my! I think my heart's stopped!"

"I fell off that roof," Boffin panted, ignoring her heart. "I was tryin' to jump from that buildin' to that other. I didn't come down graceful like 'melia Airheart." He peered into the streets ahead.

"Was it... was it always dangerous?"

"Fallin' off roofs was. And hunger could be. Many times I near starved to death. My toes froze in winter. We're nearly there." Hugging the sides of the buildings and fences, Boffin noted escape routes. "Keep in the shadows. The Persons asleep on the benches here aren't too friendly to cats." Crowds of people strolled down the streets.

"It's like daylight," Calico Cat whispered, "but..."

"It's not." They hid in shrubs bordering the park. Boffin's

whiskers were like antenna picking up danger signals. Calico Cat quivered with excitement. They rested until the shadows deepened and the streets became quieter. "Follow me fast when I run." As a car zoomed by, Boffin cried, "Now!" He dashed across the street with Calico Cat after him, her legs a blur. Boffin's eyes swivelled in every direction as he sniffed the air. "This way." He trotted quickly, hugging the buildings. Calico Cat trailed behind flicking her tail. A couple of window shoppers spotted Calico Cat and bent down to pet her.

When she caught up to Boffin, he said, "Don't be friendly with Persons. We're soon there." Calico Cat's round eyes shone. "This is the shop." They stood on their hind legs and looked into the bright interior. Vases of flowers, china, stuffed dogs and birds stood on the tables, but no calico cats. On the other side of the door there were cushions, colorful blankets, towels and linens scattered around, but still no calico cats.

"Is this the right shop?" Calico Cat asked anxiously.

"Has to be. Let's try the door." Through the glass they saw bowls, tea pots, pottery, books and candle holders with red and blue candles on tables. Shelves along the walls held various objects and strewn along the floor were cushions. "Look! Back there!" Boffin pointed.

Calico Cat moved so close to Boffin that he could feel her heart beating. She'd closed her eyes, then opened them a crack. "I can't see a thing!"

"Wait 'til your eyes get used to the light." The blurred colors on the shelves, tables, and the floor gradually became cats, a blue cat covered with yellow daisies, a yellow with green and red spots, a white figure covered with blue forget-me-nots and a green one dotted with orange marigolds. The empty eyes stared into space, without curiosity, joy or excitement. Motionless, their bodies gleamed cold and hard in the glaring light.

Calico Cat looked at the soft glow of Boffin's black coat, the three colors of her own. She turned again to the cats and stared. "Are these ..." she began, "real cal..."

Boffin sneezed. "Panther took me 'round window shoppin' and he said those are cal'co cats. Panther knew a lot."

"But I'm not... spotty like that? Do I really look like them?" Her voice was full of tears.

Boffin studied Calico Cat. "These cats aren't like us. They really... uh... belong to Persons. We don't." His voice became stronger. "Persons are useful, but we can take them or leave them, at least in the alley." What exactly had he and his friends talked about that night behind Le Chat Noir as they'd licked the butter and cream from their whiskers? They'd boasted about chasing strange cats from garbage cans, teasing dogs in the park, and even scaring the cat cousins that peered out from behind fences. But when the cold winds blew and the rain fell, they'd all silently envied the cat cousins sitting behind windows without admitting it to each other. Were calico cats and ancestors related?

Calico Cat began padding silently down the street, her head down, her tail sweeping the sidewalk.

"Let's go to *Le Chat Noir*," Boffin cried excitedly. "Probably you never ate such good food."

"I'm not hungry," Calico Cat mumbled.

"It's just 'round the corner. We'll see Mustard and Boxer and Scat-cat and Scruff and Panther..."

"I don't know them, they're only alley cats."

Boffin glared at her. "Go then. I'm goin' to *Le Chat Noir* to see my old friends and my old haunts and..."

Calico Cat turned on Boffin. "What if I get lost? A mad dog might jump out of the bushes in that park!"

Boffin stared. This wasn't the strutting Calico Cat he knew. "Come with me then, you don..."

"What will Merlinda say when she hears you left me a million miles from The Room? And Ten Lives will be shocked!"

Boffin's fur stirred. Confused, he hesitated, then began to retrace their steps to The Room.

Calico Cat trotted silently beside Boffin. Why was he going back? When at last they scrambled over the gate, The Room was dark and quiet. Without a word, Calico Cat disappeared.

Boffin was sorry that Calico Cat was disappointed but her ancestors meant nothing to him. Still a sort of restlessness trembled through him. The empty-eyed calico cats, unable to move, feel anger or happiness, haunted him. They were real prisoners. He stared into the shadowy night. The intricate thread of a spider's web gleamed faintly in the moonlight. Were there other kinds of imprisonment?

Chapter Nine

In the soft light of late afternoon, Boffin was returning to
The Room from the stream where he'd spent happy hours chasing dragon flies, frogs and butterflies. Now he was hungry. As he
stepped out of the woods, he heard Ten Lives' deep voice, "Oooh,
nooo!" The others turned in Boffin's direction. The fur on Merlinda's
back rose while Dandelion's eyes became huge circles. Kanpur
stared, not at him, Boffin realized, but behind him. He stopped
and turned. Barely out of the woods stood a dark animal with a
white stripe down its back. Boffin froze.

Out of the corner of his eye, he saw Amelia Airheart rise
slowly on her branch, creep along, and stare down. His mouth
went dry. The Woman shrieked, "No, Amelia Airheart!" But she
jumped. In mid-flight, she suddenly pushed her legs and tail stiffly
downward as though trying to brake, but down she came, down,
down, down. She landed behind Boffin, right in front of the startled
skunk. Just as the skunk's tail rose, something dashed out of the
undergrowth - Calico Cat. She screamed. Barely touching the
ground, Amelia Airheart turned and streaked back up the oak. A

sharp odor drifted like a colorless fog across the yard, piercing every nostril, stinging every eye. Boffin raced to the patio while the others scattered everywhere. The skunk disappeared into the woods.

Calico Cat, the target of the skunk's deadly salvo, wailed as she stumbled to the patio, bringing the immensity of the skunk's odor with her. Boffin crept into the corner under the couch.

"Oh, Calico Cat, why did you have to be there?" The Woman scooped her up and plunged her into one, two, three tomato juice baths. Calico Cat's screams battered Boffin's ears. When silence finally crept over the yard, the others emerged one by one. But Calico Cat's red bowl was moved from the circle. No one would go near her.

Marmeduke hissed accusingly, "Why don't you go back to the garbage cans where you belong, alley cat?"

Everyone else avoided Boffin too. "What've I done?" he moaned. "What'd I do?"

Finally Merlinda called sharply, "The skunk followed you home, Boffin." She stared straight ahead.

"But I didn't ask the critter home," Boffin cried. "I haven't never asked a skunk home for dinner."

"You're a cat, and a cat ought to know when a skunk is following it," Merlinda sighed. "Poor Calico Cat."

Boffin crept into the wood. If only he had a place like Kanpur's. Stumbling blindly along, he tripped over Calico Cat who was curled up beside a log. "How dare you come near me!" she screamed. "I never want to see you again! Never!"

Boffin backed up slowly. "Cal'co Cat, I didn't mean to... I'm real sorry you got skunk-sprayed. I didn't know it were there.

I didn't..." Then he mumbled, "The garage weren't my fault."

"Go away!" she screamed. "Just go away!"

At meals Boffin would nibble a few bites, but he could hardly swallow. He tried coming early, but when the others arrived, he choked. When he came late, his food would be gone. Probably Marmeduke was eating it again. He skipped meals now and then. His coat lost its glow, his bones began to stick out. One day The Woman said, "You're ribs are showing, Boffin, it's off to the vet's if you get any thinner." Boffin raced away. Vet White Coat's - never! He'd run away first.

Boffin hid in the bushes at the edge of the woods. He felt like crying. He was too ashamed to go near Ten Lives. He couldn't talk to Merlinda. Calico Cat sat as near her as the elder would allow. The others shouted across the yard, "Hi, Calico Cat!"

When The Woman finally said Calico Cat smelled sweet enough to join the others for breakfast, she sat staring at Amelia Airheart. "Ah.. Ah..melia Airheart...di..did you..."

Ten Lives harrumphed. "You're back, Calico Cat. Meals weren't the same without you! No, they weren't."

"I had not seen a skunk before," Kanpur said. "It is a pretty creature."

"Oh, pretty!" Marmeduke sneered.

"What did you think it was?" Calico Cat asked.

Before Amelia Airheart could reply, Marmeduke snorted, "She didn't think. Like Boffin, she never thinks."

"You ought to think before you leap," Merlinda purred.

No one spoke to Boffin, no one gave him a kind look. He slipped away to the stream. "The skunk wasn't my fault," he moaned. "Do you invite a mosquito to land on your nose?" Should he go back to the alley? But he was hungry. He'd stay for dinner, maybe even spend the night so he'd be well rested for the journey. And he might as well have breakfast before he left so he wouldn't start out hungry.

Chapter Ten

Boffin had slept badly. His red eyes opened to a grey dawn. After breakfast, which was a silent affair, he stomped down the path to the woods. His toes, ear tufts, tail, fur, even toe nails were hurts biting like fleas. Should he return to the alley? But he remembered the hungry times when his stomach had felt full of holes. "And that mean thievin' tom's still out there," he reminded himself.

But how could he stay? Just yesterday, Calico Cat again blamed him because she hadn't found her ancestors and Marmeduke was meaner than ever. "Who am I?" He started, then grumped, "I am who I am," as he tripped over a root.

Amelia Airheart looked down. "Good morning, Boffin!"

He glared up at the grey tiger face hanging over the branch. "It's mornin'!" Boffin snapped, stepping on an acorn. "Ouch! Can't you keep your path clean?" He hurried along, feeling sorrier than ever for himself. He kicked a pebble so hard that it rose high into the air, and then dropped down, down, right on Ten Lives' tail.

Ten Lives, swatting at dragon flies hovering over the pond,

leapt high in the air as the rock hit. He whipped around. Boffin hurried past the elder and was entering the wood when Ten Lives' words exploded in his ears. "You'll be back in the alley if you don't smarten up!" Boffin glanced back. Ten Lives was vigorously licking his tail. When he turned back to his dragonflies, he sputtered, "The sun isn't even sparkling on the water anymore. Could that alley cat have knocked it out of the sky?"

Boffin sank to the ground. Marmeduke always called him an 'alley cat'; Ten Lives never had before.

Merlinda hobbled up. "Don't mind Boffin, Ten Lives, he needs time to sort things out." Boffin hid under a bush to wait until she passed, but she lay down beside Ten Lives. "You need cheering yourself, Ten Lives." Scratching his ear, he grunted angrily. She continued, "Boffin's been sitting at the gate staring out for hours, his tail always dragging on the ground, even first thing in the morning."

Swatting at the water bugs still skimming over the surface, Ten Lives snapped, "That fur bag needs a good swat! Getting too big for his suit, silly ragtag that he is."

"Go easy on him," Merlinda said. "Marmeduke gives him such a rough time." Boffin's ears pricked up.

"Boffin should put that stuffed muff in his place," Ten Lives grunted. "Why Calico Cat and Dandelion hang out with him is more'n..."

"Marmeduke's flash and dash and full o' feline charm. Anyway, fighting's not Boffin's way," Merlinda sighed. "Something's bothering him. Maybe once an alley cat, always an alley cat. Leopards don't become dogs."

Ten Lives blinked. "How's that? No cat wants to become a

begging dog!"

Merlinda continued. "Boffin's bound to feel a little fenced in here."

"What's stopping that rag bag from going out nights?" Ten Lives licked his paws, then shook his whole body.

"That trip downtown stirred something deep inside Boffin's fur," Merlinda sighed. "Alley life's tough, but here, snoring on the patio is the day's excitement unless Amelia Airheart drops down. Another cat'a bowl always looks fuller than your own." She gazed at the tree tops.

"Bosh!" Ten Lives huffed. "Two square meals a day, any hobo would be grateful!"

"That holds him here, but something's bothering him. When I was young," she purred dreamily, "I had this fellow, Tom, after me."

Ten Lives glared at her. "You never told me that!"

"He left before you came. He was a big, handsome tiger, king of the neighborhood. Everyone danced to his tune."

"I wouldn't have."

She ignored his sputterings. "What a tenor voice! He crooned on the back fence, it was so romantic! I was quite smitten."

"Until he got hoarse," Ten Lives grumbled.

Lost in her glorious past, Merlinda reminisced. "Other fellows started hanging around my yard, a marmelade job that would've made Marmeduke look just plain, a blue-eyed Siamese but his eyes were crossed, and a bobcat without a tail..."

"A bobcat!" Ten Lives stared at her aghast.

"There are bobcats and bobcats," Merlinda mused. "He

was fun to be with, but unreliable. He fell through the glass roof of a greenhouse one night, and I had to sit outside the door comforting him until he got out the next morning. I felt like a potted plant." She frowned. "What a long sit that was! My fur actually began to itch. It was so frustrating sitting there with just a piece of glass between us, just sitting. I was both angry and sorry for him. I didn't know if I preferred Tom, or this fellow, getting into one adventure after another," she finished.

"Sounds more like one scrape after another to me," Ten Lives thundered. "Who...who did you choose?"

"You came along, Ten Lives," Merlinda purred. "One of those kittens I had looked a little like Tom, but two of them were exactly like you, their little pink noses just like yours!" She got up slowly. "I have to find Boffin. Don't fall into the water, Ten Lives." As she shuffled past Ten Lives, she sighed, "That mad bobcat was exciting though."

Ten Lives' eyes followed the white figure hobbling down the path. "One kitten had your grass-green eyes, Merlinda, I wanted two of you to love me, two Merlindas."

Boffin rose. Where could he find his Merlinda? He padded through the woods and nearly bumped into Dandelion who was pouncing on crickets and batting insects, smelling flowers and squinting at birds in the tree tops breaking the silence with their songs. "Boffin," she cried, "I didn't know you were here!" She leapt up to catch a butterfly, missed it, and when she landed, she went racing through the high grass. "Come, play with me, Boffin!"

There was nothing he wanted more. But if Marmeduke

were here, Dandelion would taunt him about getting crumbs on his whiskers or milk on his mustache. Soaked in his sadness from his ear tufts to his toes, he stared at the sun sifting through Dandelion's long fur, outlining her in light. "She's so beautiful," he sighed. "If only..." But he turned. "I gotta go." Head hanging, Boffin trudged through the woods.

Memories of his alley life drifted through his head. Were there really scents from Le Chat Noir in the air? There'd been no liver in cream at The Room, but neither had he had to eat mouldy bread or go hungry, except when he was late. Regular meal times, a safe place to sleep, his own bowl, sometimes The Room seemed more like prison than paradise. Aimlessly, Boffin wandered to the gate and was soon trotting down the street. He felt strangely lighter with each step. He didn't hear the roaring cars, barking dogs, and rocks thrown by people as he raced along. He didn't think about where he was going, he just kept running, farther and farther from The Room.

Chapter Eleven

Noon found Boffin in the hot dusty alley behind *Le Chat Noir*. The clatter of dishes and shouts came from the kitchen. Not one of his old friends was around. It was too early, he remembered, they'd come tonight. He could go to the river where they'd often spent hot afternoons. But the cars on the street whizzed by with such frightening speed that he felt his body tremble.

Boffin returned to the alley where he collapsed in the shade of the fence. The flies buzzed in his ears, the garbage cans smelled, and the heat pulsed. He'd forgotten this part of alley life. He sank into a troubled dream in which bits of the past floated by - Scat-cat almost flattened by a car, Scruff attacked by a dog, spilled clams in the park the day he thought he'd starve to death.

As afternoon slid into the cool stillness of evening, Boffin woke up. He rose and stretched. Suddenly he noticed three of his kind outlined against the light falling from the open back door of *Le Chat Noir*. Stiff, silent statues. A moth-eaten one-eyed tabby blinked at him. "Who're you?" The cat's voice echoed strangely in Boffin's head - "Who're you? - oo're you? - 're you?- 're you?"

"B...Boffin," he stuttered. "I.. I came.. I d..don't live here now. I..I came to say hello to Scruff."

"Who?" the cat screamed, screwing her face so the orange eye almost disappeared.

"Scruff used to come here," Boffin whispered, "and Mustard and Rarebit and Scatcat and..."

"Don't know none of them," the cat yawned, showing sharp-pointed yellow fangs. "Ain't seen none of them here. Oh, oh, here comes Jake." She turned her back to Boffin.

A huge patchy grey and black hulk swaggered toward him, frowning fiercely. Behind this monster sat a pale cat on a garbage can, its grey eyes lifeless, each rib outlined on its scrawny side. Was it alive? Suddenly a high-pitched scream shattered the stillness. Boffin whipped around. The monster was crouched, the fur on his head rising and rippling down the spine to the tip of the tail until he was outlined in fiery light. As the monster lunged, Boffin scrambled to the top of the fence.

Just then, a truck swung into the alley. As it passed, Boffin leapt into the box and landed in the middle of chickens, hundreds of them, thousands perhaps. A chorus of squawks exploded as the chickens clawed at each other to get away from him. Feathers floated everywhere. Boffin crouched in the middle of the cacklers, shaking so his suit felt like it was rattling. One after another stretched its neck out to peck at him. Boffin froze. "They're as scared of you as you are of them," his inner voice whispered. As the truck sped along, their shrieks gradually changed to squabblings of complaint. Curled into a ball, Boffin stared at their bright beady eyes through the fading light.

Darkness had fallen when the truck finally stopped. Boffin burst from the sea of chickens, who squawked another storm, to the top of the box, dropped to the ground, and raced away. His heart was pounding so hard he thought he'd break to pieces. Where was he? The voice inside his head whispered, "Miles from The Room!" How could he get back? "With your four feet." the voice suggested sensibly. Where should he go? "Follow the map inside your head.'" Then the voice added, "Better listen to me.'"

"Get goin'," Boffin muttered. Where? He'd run away from The Room. "Just move your feet, Boffin," the voice urged.

He travelled all night through a forest, black and silent except for a hooting owl and rustling in the grass. By daybreak he was exhausted. A dilapidated building in a meadow caught his eye. He stepped warily into the dusky interior and did a sniffing check before collapsing in a corner. He was asleep almost before he'd closed his eyes.

Hours later he woke to a loud thunk! thunk! thunk! Where was he? What was that noise? Slowly the events of yesterday came back. Creeping cautiously to an open window, Boffin put his paws on the sill and peered out. The trees swayed in the wind. Clouds rushed across the grey sky. A door, hanging from one hinge, was banging back and forth against the wall. Boffin jumped through the window and began running. Then stopped. Some-one was calling. "'Come on, you ragamuffins, here's breakfast."

The Woman's voice! His stomach growled. The birds were beginning to warble around him. He was deep in the forest, miles from The Room... why was he thinking about The Room? He started forward again. "I don't belong there, I like bein' alone," he mumbled. Of course if he were there now, he'd soon be eating.

"Don't think about your stomach," the voice scolded.

"That's okay for you," Boffin snapped, "you probably don't ever eat." The words seemed to hang in the air before dissolving. "It's so quiet it feels weird," he muttered. Something chattered. A squirrel was eyeing him. "Get lost," he hissed.

By late afternoon Boffin was desperately hungry. There was a gurgling sound... a stream perhaps? He raced toward it. In a small meadow was a pool from which a tiny stream trickled. He lapped greedily until he burped loudly.

Boffin continued slowly now, padding steadily all night. Merlinda's eyes flashed before him, gazing steadily at him. "Rubbish!" he snapped. The next morning, he sank under a shrub and again slept until late afternoon. When he woke, he lay with his eyes closed, aware of every aching muscle in his body. And the pads of his feet were sore. But wait. He wasn't alone. He cracked open one eye. Then both eyes popped wide. In front of him stood a porcupine with three young ones, staring at him. Boffin stared back. The mother was very big. Were they hungry? Did they eat cats? He'd better get out of here. But the mother turned and, followed by her family, waddled down the path in a swaying fat line. Boffin sighed hugely. "Gotta get goin'."

The voice spoke now and then. "Go into that farm yard." There he found some food in a bowl, dog-food but "Beggars can't be..." He turned suddenly. Two dogs were dashing toward him, barking. Out of the door tore a man, a gun in his hand. Boffin streaked to the barn, leapt to the rail fence and raced along it before dropping into the tall grass just as a deafening bang shattered the air. He sped along until the dogs' voices faded. Then he collapsed, gasping for breath. "You'll live," the voice assured him.

After a short rest, Boffin came to another stream, wide and clear. He drank deeply. The voice urged, "Follow the bank for a little way." Around the bend, a fallen tree reached nearly across the stream. "Cross here," the voice commanded. As he jumped from a limb on the far side, it broke and down he plunged into the water. The swift current swept him along. Struggling to keep his head up, Boffin reached desperately for a log floating by, hooked his claws into the wood and clambered up. Straddling the log, he rode it for several hours down the stream, remembering Rarebit who'd nearly drowned once. 'Unload the memories, keep your wits sharp!' the voice scolded. Boffin stared ahead. His log was fast approaching another tree lying across the stream. He crouched. Just as the log hit it, he leapt off. "What timing! What a nimble fellow you are!" he told himself. "I sure look like a drowned rat now, but my sore pads really liked that ride!" He shook himself. The voice was silent.

As the light faded, he began shivering. "Boffin, you need a place to sleep," he muttered, "and don't tell me...is that really..." There stood a barn in the middle of a hay field. Up the ladder to the loft he struggled, then curled in the hay and fell fast asleep. Hours later he woke, hungry now, but rested. He'd make good time today. But wait, something moved in the hay. He locked his eyes on the spot. Suddenly, a mouse scurried across the loft. Boffin raced after it. It scurried one way, then another. He pounced, missed, then bounded to the front of the loft where it disappeared over the edge. Boffin sprang after it, right out of the loft into a hay wagon that was passing below. The voice purred, "You're getting lucky." Boffin settled down for a ride to wherever. "But I lost my breakfast." His stomach ached. "Lucky mouse," the voice chirped. "Humph!" Boffin snorted. He'd eaten mice in the alley but only when he'd found nothing else. Now, as his stomach screamed for food, he recalled another strategy he'd used when he'd been hungry - "Don't think about it." He tried that now. Buried in the soft hay at the back of the wagon, he crooned, "Real comfort this, will it carry me all the way home?" Home? Where was that? Before he could decide, the wagon came to a stop and he leapt off.

Boffin drank water from streams and mud puddles, and ate mice and birds when he caught them. "Food to keep me from starvin' before I get home," he excused himself. "Goin' home, I'm goin' home," he hummed off key. And where is home? "Don't confuse yourself with details," he chided himself, and croaked, "Oh, I've miles to go, miles to go, and my feet are awful sore!" They were. His muscles ached and the emptiness gnawed holes inside. "I wonder if Cal'co Cat was this starved after three days in the garage." He wished she were here to talk to now. But he'd run away - from her? - to be alone? He couldn't remember.

Days blurred into nights. He often stopped to sleep because he was drowning in weariness. "Which way should I go?" he mumbled as his red eyes opened. The voice was silent. "You're coming home..." he heard. He blinked; wasn't that Merlinda's voice? He padded forward, then stopped. Red sky - was it morning or evening? His cut feet bled. His fur was dirty and matted. "You're a walkin' mess!" he giggled, "and gettin' daffy, talkin' to yourself." But he'd always done that. Sometimes he wandered in circles. His spirits wobbled. "Just one more day," he'd coax his worn body after a brief rest. "Maybe we'll reach The Room tomorrow, Feet," he'd whisper hoarsely as he licked the sore pads. "Or the next day." If only. "Wonder what Dand'line's doin'? And Ten Lies..." His eyes watered. They felt sunburned. The voice finally spoke: "You're making good time." That was the day he thought every step would be his last.

Before dawn began lighting the sky the next morning, Boffin recognized a maple beside the stream. "I've climbed that tree many a time," he cried excitedly. "I've reached the park." The fog swirling through his mind thinned. *Le Chat Noir* had to be near. Now he could find his way back to The Room. The Room? No, no, his friends might be at *Le Chat Noir* by this time, he had to go there.

Boffin was about to dash over the grass to the street when he stopped abruptly. Across the meadow at the edge of the woods stood a slate-grey cat glaring at him. The vicious tom. It took a step forward, then stopped. The black-slitted yellow eyes drilled into Boffin as the Shadow began circling the meadow with long slow strides.

Boffin watched, aware now that energy was seeping into his weary muscles. "Don't let it get on your back and watch your throat," he reminded himself. Fearlessly, it moved closer. Boffin's eyes narrowed. "It must have followed me to The Room," Boffin muttered. "Bet that's what 'melia Airheart saw that day." Closer and closer the Shadow came, slowly yet steadily striding along the edge of the woods, its eyes locked on him.

Boffin rose to his full height and began a stiff-legged walk into the open. Hair raised on his hunched back, fangs hanging out, deep thunder rumbling in his throat, he waited for his opponent's next move. The Shadow stopped. They circled each other now like two prize fighters, glaring eyes never wavering, angry snarls growing louder and louder. As the circles became smaller, they ripped the air with their claws. Suddenly Boffin pounced. But the Shadow leapt aside in a flash, twisted in midair, and lunged at Boffin. Landing on his back, the Shadow thrust his head forward. His white teeth flashed in the sunlight before they sank into black fur. Boffin clawed his way out. He whipped around. With lightening speed, he slashed the Shadow's shoulder. Screaming in pain, the Shadow leapt on Boffin and wrapped his arms around him. A heap of grey and black fur, they rolled across the ground. First one was on top, then the other. Boffin felt his strength draining away. He pinned the Shadow to the ground, but the grey figure slipped out and rushed at Boffin, knocking him down. Their screams were muffled as they sank their teeth into fur and flesh.

The wounds spurted blood, covering their coats with dark, wet splotches. Boffin pulled free but his quivering legs collapsed. When teeth closed around his throat, he pushed weakly. A blurry form flashed by as the teeth loosened. From a distance, he heard a hoarse whisper, "Dirty Socks! You ain't dead, are you?" Then everything went black.

Boffin woke up. He was lying in a blanket-lined box. His body ached, his muscles felt sore, pain throbbed everywhere. Images floated by - chickens, a log, rushing water, a red sun, flashing fangs... "The fight!" he whispered hoarsely. He tried to stand, but fell back. His eyes darted around. He was alive, but where was he?

"Ah, you've come to!" a deep voice boomed. A Man stomped over and towered above him. "You was near a gonner when I found you, sonny. Tough little mutt, ain't you? I reckon you'll be fine in a few days." Boffin couldn't keep his eyes open.

For many days he slept and woke and dreamed grey fog until finally he surrendered to it. He was lifted up, rose up, up until he soared over the trees, high above the river. Below him the white-capped chef of *Le Chat Noir* threw a piece of liver into bubbling butter. The aroma swirled up in a blue smoke to his nose. As he put out his tongue to lap the scent, he suddenly found himself tumbling head over tail, down, down. He landed with a thump and bounced several times on the hard ground.

A tree was growing out of the street in front of the tobacco shop around the corner from *Le Chat Noir*. It grew so quickly it soon towered above the other trees, and still it kept growing up, up, up. Boffin leapt onto a branch and ran along it. Above him, gooseberry green cat's eyes stared down at him, first from behind one clump of leaves, then from behind another. "Wait for me!" he called. Up he climbed, higher and higher, but the eyes were always above him. Now stars twinkled through the leaves. He climbed and climbed, but he never reached the top.

He padded along a thick branch to its tip. Far below him blinked street lights. The houses and cars looked like flies. A cloud floated nearby. He crouched, leapt, and soared high above the tree, so high that the stars were all around him. Far below the cloud drifted, snow-white against the blackness. He began to float down, down and suddenly he landed in the middle of the cloud. He sank into its fluffy softness, rose to the surface, and then lay quite still.

The stars seemed near enough to touch. He reached out, but they moved beyond his paw. Was that a cat grinning at him? Above it stood another with its tail pointing up while all around others were sitting, jumping or washing. But what was up and what was down? They seemed to move down when they leapt and back up to land. A white cat, her eyes grass-green, leaned toward him and whispered, "You must come home... come home... come home..."

He sat up. "Home? Where is home?" he called. But the white cat had faded from view. He whipped around. A brown cat sat on the edge of the cloud, her gold eyes bright beacons. Was she smiling at him? Before he could say anything, she rose, and crouched. "Wait!" he screamed, but she jumped. Tears streamed down his face as he ran to the edge where she'd stood. He scanned the darkness. Far below him, floating like a feather caught in a gentle breeze, was the brown cat, drifting farther and farther away until she became a mere speck. She landed lightly, glanced up at him, and raced across a green field. Suddenly his cloud began to disappear. Before he had time to flick his tail, he leapt off the cloud and somersaulted down, twirling faster and faster until bang! he hit the ground.

Boffin's eyes snapped open. The Man was standing above him. He bent down and scratched Boffin's head roughly. "Yeah, you're lucky I found you. I need a good mouser. This'll be a good home for you."

Boffin shrank from his touch. His eyes swept the room. How could he escape?

As the days passed, Boffin ate and felt himself grow stronger. Fragments of the dream drifted past him - the voice whispering, "'Your must come home...home...'" "Merlinda's voice!" he cried. He thought he saw gooseberry green eyes shining through the leaves of the tree outside the window, and Amelia Airheart's face flashed before him. One afternoon, as he hung between sleep and waking, the gold-eyed brown cat floated off the cloud. Boffin jumped. "Kanpur!" he shouted. She wasn't here, yet he trembled at her nearness. "And I have a message for Cal'co Cat!" Something about the stars, but what? He lay quivering. Then his mind strayed to the alley, but he saw only a blank screen.

One day when The Man stepped out to get his mail, Boffin crept up behind him. As soon as the door swung open, he slipped out so quickly that The Man didn't notice him until he'd leapt to the top of the fence. "Hey, come back, Cat! Get back here you little monster!" Boffin heard as he dashed across the grass.

Boffin raced into the park, and stopped. The Shadow might still be there. But what he stumbled upon stunned him.

He followed the stream to the bridge where he planned to cross the street. Something lying under a shrub near the water caught Boffin's eye. Matted dirty fur lay loosely over bones jutting out in every direction. Boffin went closer. A cat. The eyes opened and its head lifted. "Dirty Socks!" it whispered hoarsely. "You look good!" It coughed. "Tough as always, ain't you?"

Boffin stared. "Scruff! Scruff, is it really... I looked for you. What's wrong? You're sick! I'll help..."

"Yeah, don't feel so good. Reckon this is it. But we had good times together, ain't we, Dirty Socks?" He moaned softly. "I happened along just in time so we got our last fight together, me'un you. Reckon you would've been a goner." His raspy breathing pierced Boffin. "Ain't so strong as I was but I wasn't goin' to let that monster kill me pal. Don't reckon he's gonna come back."

Boffin sank down beside Scruff. "You saved my life, Scruff. I'll look after you." But there wasn't much he could do. Boffin's alley died with Scruff that night. He rose and padded away.

Boffin began to run. Pictures flashed across his mind - Scruff's broken body, the ruffians behind *Le Chat Noir*, Kanpur leaping off a cloud. "Memories can be just a bag of tricks," he puffed. The Room too was a memory, had it disappeared? But the dream was real, wasn't it? Terror gripped Boffin's throat as he tore along. "The dream's real, I'm sure of that," he repeated. A final effort propelled him to the top of the gate. His eyes searched the dark forms in the grey morning light - The Room, the oak tree, Merlinda's apple tree...all were here. His fear dropped like a cloak.

No one was up yet. Boffin tumbled into the yard. He'd go to Kanpur, she'd be awake. And he had to talk to Calico Cat and Merlinda, but they'd be asleep yet.

Kanpur's eyes shone in the dark opening of the barrel as Boffin approached her hideout. "Kanpur," he whispered.

"Who is there?" Kanpur stuck her nose out. "Is that you, Boffin? Have you returned?"

He collapsed in a heap. "Yeah. I've been runnin'..."

"Whatever for? Was someone after you?"

"Yeah, I was chasin' myse.." He stopped. "I mean..."

"You were running from yourself." Kanpur studied him.

Boffin gazed fondly at Kanpur's little round nose, her delicate whiskers. His eyes dropped to his toe sock, his ankle sock. He sneezed twice. "Kind of funny. Cal'co Cat runnin' to find herself and I runnin' from myself, I had to go back to the alley. I'd got lost here."

"Did you not recognize your reflection in the pond?"

"Never looked. When I came here, all I could think was a sure meal's enough. But with the rules and all, I began to feel sort of trapped. I missed doin' what I wanted when I wanted. And Marm'duke made fun of me and even Cal'co Cat and Dand'line didn't like so much havin' me around. And worse than not fittin' in, I wasn't happy bein' alone here like I used to be in the alley. "

"Boffin, I saw you come home!" Merlinda stepped out of the woods, her figure stark white against the shadows.

Boffin glanced at her shyly. "Merlinda, I... I hope you didn't worry... I mean, I guess you didn't..."

"Boffin, if I told you my fur ached, my teeth itched, sleep didn't sooth and food was tasteless while you were gone, would you believe me?" .

Boffin noted the twinkle in her eyes. "I'm sorry, but when I left, I felt like that skunk that followed me home so I started thinkin' nobody wanted this Boffin around here and then I wondered, who is he? My friend Scruff would've said, `I'm just a moth-eaten mess o' fur!' That made me laugh even when I was cryin' on the inside."

Merlinda sighed. "But your friend's a wise one."

"Yeah. I thought I had to go back because I must have left the real Boffin in the alley."

"You found something on your quest," Kanpur observed.

"My alley's gone. Scruff's dead and everything seems wrong. Well, different. Even *Le Chat Noir* isn't the same."

Merlinda sighed. "Yes, familiar signposts disappear and we have to find new ones."

"Yeah, it's somethin' like that for sure. I should have known that when I couldn't get all of you out of my head."

"But you belonged when you returned with Calico Cat."

"I knew if I let Cal'co Cat come back alone, and somethin' happened to her, your eyes would always follow me. I never knew they'd follow me when I ran away."

"The way you see is what you see," Merlinda purred.

Boffin cried, "The dream told me you two are the new signposts because you told me to come home, Merlinda, and you led me here, Kanpur!" Merlinda's green eyes twinkled; Kanpur's were deep golden pools. His own felt misty. If only it were raining, the tears would look like rain drops, but the sky was a cloudless blue.

"We are," Kanpur said, "if you think we are."

Boffin continued. "I have to tell Cal'co Cat about the star map in the sky! Do you miss India, Kanpur?"

"India is with me. I carry it around inside this suit. Of course fur is only on the outside," Kanpur said softly.

"That's a fact," Boffin agreed, "and a good thing too, because it'd be mighty cold without it in winter. But when it's too hot, I'd like to take it off. How would I look without my fur suit!"

Kanpur's eyes sparkled, and Merlinda's purr sounded like a chuckle. Boffin felt warm inside. They sank into the stillness that filled the meadow as the sun rose over the trees, bathing their world in gold. Merlinda broke the silence. "Let's go to breakfast. The Woman kept putting your bowl out, Boffin."

"And Marmeduke didn't touch it," Kanpur added.

He was stunned. "Marm'duke didn't.... I... I'll...I need sleep badly. Don't tell them I'm back, not just yet."

"As you please," Kanpur said. "Come, Merlinda, We'll make sure Marmeduke doesn't eat your breakfast, Boffin."

Chapter Twelve

"For those who like that sort of thing, that is the sort of thing they like." Merlinda's voice floated into Boffin's dream. He opened his eyes. He'd fallen asleep under the shrub after breakfast which he'd eaten when the others had already left the patio. The fur clan was gathering at the pond. Would they be happy to see him? Probably not Marmeduke. Nose on paws, Boffin eyed the scene.

"I did not know that Merlinda is a poet," Kanpur said to Calico Cat who was lying beside her.

"She's not," Marmeduke yawned from one of the hillocks. "That's Gertie Steinway. Merlinda often quotes others."

"And who is Gertie Steinway?" Kanpur asked.

"She's...ah..ah..she's..." Marmeduke stuttered as he rolled over and over until his feet hit the water.

"Marmeduke is Marmeduke is Marmeduke," Merlinda sighed.

"Is that Gertie Steinway?" Kanpur asked.

"No, that's Marmeduke," Ten Lives rumbled, awakened

by sprinkles falling on his nose.

Dandelion came galloping up, her whiskers twitching. "My food's been eaten," she gasped.

Boffin lifted his head.

Calico Cat's eyes swivelled around. "Don't blame me."

Dandelion stared at her. "You did it! Only the guilty deny something before they're accused."

"Now Dandelion," Ten Lives' deep voice thundered, "stealing is a serious crime. Consider the facts before you point a paw at someone."

Dandelion's eye now fell on Marmeduke dashing around on the bank, flicking his tail. "Marmeduke! You did it! You ate Boffin's food when he was here."

Boffin's stomach twitched uneasily.

Marmeduke stared at Dandelion. "What?"

"Marmeduke looks guilty when he's innocent," Kanpur observed.

"And innocent when he's guilty," Calico Cat added.

"You're a pig!" Dandelion cried. "You always eat..."

"Don't pronounce judgement until you have the evidence to prove guilt," Merlinda scolded.

"Maybe Boffin sneaked back and ate it!" Marmeduke said.

The fur rippled along Boffin's back; had he eaten it?

"A pig isn't a fox, and a fox isn't a pig," Merlinda purred.

"What's that supposed to mean?" Marmeduke squeaked.

Ten Lives yawned. "Those who get to meals on time don't get their food stol...er...ate...eaten."

"We should watch for the thief," Calico Cat suggested, "hide behind the house or in Amelia Airheart's tree or..."

Marmeduke's face brightened. "Yes! Catch the culprit sneaking up! We can take turns. I'll keep watch first."

Dandelion gasped, "Put the fox in the chicken coop?"

"Let Marmeduke take the first watch, Merlinda sighed.

Boffin flicked the tip of his tail uneasily.

"Then I'll go to Amelia Airheart's perch right now," Marmeduke said. "We can see everything from there."

Calico Cat reasoned, "Dandelion's food's gone. No use going up there until dinner time, Marmeduke."

Marmeduke swished his tail impatiently. "I have to find the best spot on Amelia Airheart's branch to see from. There are a lot of leaves blocking the view up there."

Ten Lives thundered, "You get dizzy standing on a chair, how're you going to be up there?"

Marmeduke strolled away mouthing, "Here I go, into the wild blue yonder..."

The others stared at bees buzzing around the roses, the water bugs skipping over the pond and a couple of crickets.

Boffin quietly sat up. From Kanpur's hideout, he'd gone to the patio. Everyone had eaten except Dandelion obviously. He'd shoved his nose into the first bowl of food he'd come to and gobbled it all before he noticed that the bowl wasn't his. His orange bowl still had food in it, so he'd eaten that too. Stuffed to his ear tufts, he'd come here, crawled under a bush, and slept soundly until Merlinda's voice awakened him. Should he walk out and confess that he'd eaten Dandelion's food by mistake? Marmeduke would call him a thief, but would Dandelion forgive him? Sick with anxiety, he watched Calico Cat saunter to a rock, roll around on it, settle on her back, and gaze upside down out of her black patched eye and her orange patched eye at the sparkling waters of the pond. "The world looks different."

Kanpur said, "Your mind sees it differently then."

Calico Cat sat up. "How, Kanpur?"

"I cannot explain it to you," Kanpur replied, looking at something in the oak. "You must study your mind's movements." Just then, a shriek pierced the air. Everyone jumped up and raced towards The Room. Boffin stepped out.

"The thief's been caught! The thief's been caught!" Dandelion yelled as she reached the patio. But only eight empty bowls sat in the sun.

"Look!" Kanpur pointed at the oak. Every eye travelled up the trunk, along the heavy limb to Amelia Airheart's perch, across a leafy patch, and stopped. Amelia Airheart stared down at a pear-shaped orange body swinging to and fro from the limb. It was Marmeduke. His eyes looked like extra-large egg yolks with a black streak down each center.

"Get me down from here!" Marmeduke screamed.

Boffin, who'd trailed behind, saw Amelia Airheart bend over Marmeduke. "You have only one choice. If you don't have the strength to pull yourself up, just let go. You'll reach the ground in no time," she finished encouragingly.

"How did that happen, Marmeduke?" Dandelion shouted, dashing around the base of the tree.

Marmeduke's eyes rolled down. "Ohhh," he groaned, "Dandelion's the size of a mouse! You want me to break my legs," he accused Amelia Airheart.

"Our kind don't usually break our legs when we jump, unless you hit something," Amelia Airheart comforted him, "like a tree stump or Dandelion, but I expect she'd get the worst of it." Marmeduke looked even more terrified.

Boffin, standing behind the group, glanced at everyone before slowly rolling his eyes up until he reached Marmeduke swaying gently back and forth, an agonized look on his face. "Oh Marm'duke," Boffin called casually, "you're hangin' from the limb of the oak tree." Marmeduke glared at him.

"Boffin, you're back!" Everyone crowded around him and began to talk at once. "I never thought we'd see you again!" - "Were you lost?" - "Did you miss us?" Friendly purrs filled the air. Ten Lives' nose touched Boffin's, Calico Cat's side rubbed against him, and Dandelion licked his ear. "How'd Marm'duke get up there?"

"He climbed up the trunk," Amelia Airheart called helpfully.

"He's trying to catch whoever stole Dandelion's breakfast," Calico Cat explained.

"We're taking turns," Dandelion began, but Boffin interrupted.

"Hangin' from the tree?"

"Help me to get out of this!" Marmeduke screamed.

Boffin looked at his grey socks. "D..D..Dand'lion," he stammered, "I've somethin' to tell you." He tried to go on but he couldn't find his voice.

Everyone stared at him. "Boffin, what's the matter, you look like you're going to cry!" Calico Cat cried.

Boffin's eyes filled with tears. "I'm afraid you won't forgive me." He paused. "I... I ate your breakfast. I... I didn't mean to do it." He stared down, his voice trembled. "I was so hungry I gobbled it all down before I saw it was your pink bowl, and then I ate my breakfast because I was really starved." He glanced up.

Dandelion looked stunned. "Two breakfasts! You ate two breakfasts! I'm still hungry."

"A real thief doesn't confess," Merlinda said.

Now everyone spoke at once - "Where were you, Boffin?" - "How'd you get so dirty?" - "Did you eat when you were gone, you're so skinny!" - "Why did you stay away so long?"

Boffin told them about his ride with the chickens, about the porcupine family, being chased by dogs now the size of bears and shot at by their master, the ride down the swirling stream on a log. They gasped and stared at him with admiration and affection as they listened. A moan drifted down from the limb above their heads. Boffin looked up. He thought he loved even Marmeduke at this moment. "It wasn't nothin' really," he murmured, wiggling his toes. "The alley was different from what I remember. Nothin' to eat and my friends were gone. But you all were in my head."

Marmeduke groaned, "Have you forgotten me?"

The cat clan took their eyes off Boffin and looked up. "The problem seems to be one of coming down," Ten Lives thundered, "but what goes up must come down."

"But what comes down doesn't have to get up," Calico Cat suggested.

"Unless it's a balloon," Dandelion said cheerfully.

"Balloons soar ever so high," Calico Cat reminded her, "and Marmeduke can't do that."

"Don't!" Marmeduke screamed, his eyes tightly closed.

"No, Marm'duke, you don't want to do that," Boffin agreed, sitting down again. "You're kind of heavy for that."

"But you have really distinct rings on your tail, Marmeduke," Calico Cat called.

"Distinctive," Kanpur said.

Dandelion gazed admiringly at his tail. "Distinctly rings, like a raccoon's! They're gorgeous, Marmeduke!"

Boffin turned his head to look at his own tail. "My black rope ain't near as handsome as your ringed job, Marm'duke. Maybe if I had spots or stripes," he said wistfully, eyeing his dusty tail. Suddenly he remembered that the admired tail belonged to Marmeduke who was still dangling from the branch. Boffin blinked at the pear shape. Marmeduke didn't look nearly as comfortable as he felt. But how to help Marmeduke feel better was a greater problem than his plain tail, he knew. "I'd trade tails with you if I could, Marm'duke!" Marmeduke groaned in terror. Boffin turned to the others. "We ought to do somethin'."

Amelia Airheart called, "I've told Marmeduke what to do, but he won't listen to me, or at least he won't do it."

Merlinda now spoke. "I have an idea. We must all stand below Marmeduke and be ready to catch him when he lets go of the branch. That way, we'll each have to catch just a little bit of him." Everyone blinked in agreement. Marmeduke looked doubtful, but no one asked for his opinion.

"Merlinda," Ten Lives said anxiously, "you stand back and direct the operation. Then we'll work together better."

"Okay," Merlinda agreed. "On one, all of you get into a circle below Marmeduke. On two, put your paws up, and on three, Marmeduke, you must let go." Amelia Airheart moved back without taking her eyes off Marmeduke. Merlinda looked up. "Ready?" Marmeduke's eyes were tightly closed.

"Keep your claws in!" Boffin yelled.

"One!" Merlinda began. Everyone formed a circle below Marmeduke. "Two!" Their arms stretched up, paws turned to the sky, claws withdrawn. "Three!" They closed their eyes. And waited. And waited. And waited.

"Where's Marmeduke?" Dandelion finally cried. "Did he run away?" Everyone's eyes popped open and swept the yard.

"Nope, the fur bag's still here," Amelia Airheart assured them. Marmeduke was still swinging gently back and forth, his eyes tightly closed.

"Marmeduke," Calico Cat called, "you can open your eyes, you're still up in the tree, high above the ground."

"Oh, stop it! Stop it! I can't be!" Marmeduke cried, opening his eyes a crack. "Oh, yes, I am, I see I am, I suppose I forgot to let go."

"Try lettin' go with one paw before we begin," Boffin suggested.

"No! No!" Marmeduke screamed. "I mean," he muttered gruffly, "I won't forget to let go this time."

"Okay. One!" Merlinda began counting. Again the rescue basket formed. "Two!" All arms lifted. "Three!" Merlinda shouted. Again every eye closed. Plunk! Splat! Unk! Groan! Everyone looked up. Amelia Airheart was looking down. Marmeduke, sprawled on the ground, looked like a teddy bear with its stuffing knocked out. The pile of fur didn't move, but the eyes were rolling in their sockets. Merlinda shoved her nose in his face. "Are you alive or are you dead?"

An ear twitched. The eyes stopped rolling. A toe wiggled. Marmeduke squeaked, "Am I on the ground?"

"You are not in heaven," Kanpur said, batting his tail with her paw.

"You did it," Boffin said, half-admiringly.

"I don't know how it happened," Marmeduke grunted, his voice a little stronger. "I must have landed on my paws." He licked each pad in turn. "They're sore, like the time they got squeezed in the door."

Boffin noticed Merlinda gazing up at Amelia Airheart who was sitting directly above them, grooming herself carefully. Their eyes met briefly. Then Amelia Airheart stretched, and padded to her favorite spot. "Not everyone is at home in trees," he heard her murmur as she settled herself for the day to watch and listen to the birds.

The cat clan, now exhausted, sprawled in the sun around the pond and dreamed or reflected about the wonders of nature and of courage. Ten Lives again asked Boffin about his trip to the alley and made him promise never to run away again. "I didn't sleep a wink during the whole time you were gone!" he claimed. From the couch, Marmeduke snored mightily.

Chapter Thirteen

Summer had slipped into autumn. The yard was aflame with reds and purples, bronzes and golds. Before dawn, Ten Lives lay wide-eyed, gazing at the tree tops. Boffin snored gently near him. The deep blush of dawn had washed The Room, the woods, the two cats' faces crimson by the time Boffin opened his eyes.

"Not good, not good," Ten Lives rumbled.

"Why, Ten Lies?" Boffin blinked sleepily.

"Red at sunset's okay, I just don't care for red in the morning." Silently they lay side by side, watching the changing light, listening to the early birds.

Kanpur was doing her yoga. From a tall upside down U, she sank and stretched her front legs forward, pushing her rear end high in the air. Dandelion gazed in wonder at the length of time she held each pose.

Calico Cat padded around the corner of The Room, followed by a half-awake Amelia Airheart. Then Marmeduke stumbled over from the path. All sat quietly waiting for breakfast. Ten Lives looked around anxiously. Calico Cat stopped washing. "Is anything wrong, Ten Lives?"

"Have you seen Merlinda this morning, Calico Cat?"

"No, she wasn't lying on her cushion under the apple tree. Let me look again." She returned frowning. "She's not there. Is anything wrong?"

"I hope not." Ten Lives' rumbling voice shook a little. "She wasn't feeling good yesterday. Fact is, she hasn't been herself for some time."

Soon everyone was eating except Ten Lives. They finished their breakfasts and wandered off. Finally Ten Lives rose. If Merlinda hadn't come now, she wouldn't be coming. He hobbled off to look for her. Boffin tagged behind. "Amelia Airheart, have you seen Merlinda today?"

Amelia Airheart peered through the leaves. "No, I haven't seen her for several days."

"She could've seen Merlinda," Ten Lives muttered, continuing down the path. "She doesn't notice much."

Kanpur was back in her hideout. As Ten Lives and Boffin approached, she was lying just inside the barrel, eyeing a spider weaving its web outside her door. She looked about to swat it when she saw the two cats. Folding her paws, she quickly assumed her meditative pose. "Have you seen Merlinda, Kanpur?" Ten Lives asked.

Kanpur opened wide her half-closed eyes. "Yes, she has gone to the burning bush beside the stream."

"Did...did you talk to her?" Ten Lives stammered.

"Yes, we had a very long talk."

"She wasn't feeling so good yesterday."

"No, she is moving on."

"What do you mean, she's moving on?" he demanded.

Kanpur spoke quietly. "Are you not yourself on your tenth life? Merlinda is dying."

Ten Lives looked sharply at Kanpur. "She just wasn't feeling good, that's all. Why do you say she's going to die? We get colds, and the colds go away, we get stomach aches, and the stomach aches go away..."

"Thank the spirits they do go away," she sighed.

Ten Lives stared straight ahead at the trees, at the grass, at the air. He saw nothing. "The sky was red this morning," he mumbled miserably.

"Merlinda is very old, Ten Lives," Kanpur said gently. "She knows it is time, she is ready to go."

"I'm not ready for her to go," Ten Lives stammered. "I...I don't know how I'm going to live without her. She's been my companion for many years. She understands me, cares for me. She's the only one who really...who knows what we're all about. I...I need her."

Kanpur said nothing. She followed the autumn leaves drifting down before catching Boffin's eye as he sat quietly studying her. He could see that Kanpur felt Ten Lives' misery.

"Merlinda came here yesterday. She wants to see you."

Ten Lives stared at the ground. "I'll go of course, but I don't know what to say."

"You do not need to say anything," Kanpur said, gazing at the tree tops swaying gently in the morning light. "You must just go and be with her."

Boffin followed a stumbling Ten Lives through the woods. "Seems like yesterday that I met Merlinda," Ten Lives, his voice full of tears, cried as memories of the past mingled with the present. "I remember the day I chased the birds and I lost one because I opened my mouth to get a better grip. But I caught another. The Woman was angry when I dropped it at her feet, and Merlinda ignored me. Then she beckoned me to follow her into the woods. She sat down and I sat down and for a long time, she was silent, not saying a word, ignoring me, her nose in the air, her eyes half open." Ten Lives stopped. He turned to the tree tops, gazed at yesterday, perhaps. Boffin waited.

"'Listen,' Merlinda said. I listened. The forest rang with the songs of the birds, chattering squirrels, chirping crickets, the gurgling stream. 'I caught a bird once,' she said, 'a tiny bird. I killed it while I was trying to grasp it in my mouth. I tried to get it to move again, but it wouldn't. And it wouldn't sing again.' Then she walked away." Half-crying, half-laughing, Ten Lives finished, "If Merlinda had been a bird, she would have been an owl. I told her that. She said I would've been a crow because I talk so much."

Boffin was barely aware of the autumn scents, ripe apples, burning leaves, dry grass as he followed the old cat whose sorrow he felt as keenly as though he were inside Ten Lives' fur.

The brilliant red of the burning bush suddenly exploded in front of them. The two cats stopped. Under it lay Merlinda, her white body curled into a ball, every bone in her back plainly visible. "You look so small!" Ten Lives gasped. "I want to lie beside you, put my arms around you, and warm you." The light streaming through the leaves danced with the shadows in dappled rhythm across the clearing. A song sparrow's notes broke the stillness, followed by the trill of a thrush. "Merlinda's birds," the old cat whispered, glancing at the tree tops.

Boffins's eyes followed Ten Lives as he padded quietly up to Merlinda, sat down and gazed down at her thin body.

Merlinda opened her eyes. "Ten Lives, you've come. I did so want to see you one last time."

Her eyes were green as ever, green as the grass, green as the first time   Boffin had seen them. Ten Lives put his nose gently against hers. "You've been chewing that garlic plant again," Merlinda scolded.

"Oh, Merlinda!" Ten Lives gasped, burying his nose in his furry side. But he lowered himself stiffly, and lay down beside her. His paws mingled with hers. He nuzzled her ear. "I always said you had the softest ears."

Merlinda touched his paw with her nose. "I'm about to leave you, Ten Lives. And don't you go crying all over your fur, you have such a time drying it. Don't mind, life has been kind to me." Silently she lay beside Ten Lives who'd buried his nose in her side. "We've been lucky, you and I, lucky that The Woman found us, that we had each other. Don't be sad, Ten Lives." She was silent for a long time, then whispered, "I'm sorry I growled at you the first time I saw you. I was really glad to see you. I thought you'd make a better playmate than The Woman."

Ten Lives nuzzled her ear. A dim light shone from her tired eyes. "Oh, Merlinda," was all he could murmur.

Merlinda turned to the tree tops. "I can't imagine this place without you, Ten Lives." She closed her eyes, breathing so quietly that the gentle rise and fall of her side wasn't visible. Just when he thought that she'd gone to sleep, Merlinda whispered softly. "Ten Lives, did you know..." But she never finished the thought.

Ten Lives bent his head and touched noses with Merlinda for the last time. Then he lay motionless, lost in the stillness as the light grew brighter and brighter, as the day grew warmer and warmer. When the light faded, Ten Lives roused himself. Slowly he stretched the kinks out of his joints and padded stiff-legged across the clearing. Boffin, who'd waited for him, rose as Ten Lives approached. The old cat stopped, touched Boffin's nose with his own, and then continued down the path.

All the residents, even Amelia Airheart, were lying near the patio when Ten Lives and Boffin appeared.

"Merlinda seems to be here," Calico Cat whispered.

"She never left." Ten Lives' voice was so soft that the others turned to see who'd spoken.

"Merlinda may have left her body," Kanpur said, "but she is not nothing - in a manner of speaking."

"What is she then?" Dandelion asked.

Kanpur hesitated. "When the body is of no more use, we move on. It is not the end."

"People throw dead cats in the dump; the rats probably eat us," Boffin said.

"Oh, Boffin, stop!" Dandelion shuddered.

Marmeduke frowned. "Lulu, a gorgeous Persian I met last night, told me there's a cemetery for pets."

Dandelion cried, "I want to go where there are fields and fields of green daisies and pink butterflies!"

"I'll soar high in the air," Amelia Airheart said, gazing at the clouds stained pink and red and orange.

"You're here, Amelia Airheart," Ten Lives blinked. "Merlinda would like that."

"Maybe you'll have wings like the birds," Calico Cat said. "Maybe all our wishes come true when we die."

Marmeduke cried, "I want my wishes now!"

"A bowl full of food and all of you - I don't need more than that," Boffin said.

"But we do come back again and again," Kanpur mused.

"Sounds like going in circles," Calico Cat said.

"Cycles," Kanpur corrected her, "not circles."

"What's the difference?" Marmeduke asked.

Kanpur gazed at the fiery sky. "If you do not understand, I cannot tell you."

"Maybe bein' born is spring and livin' is summer and gettin' old is autumn and dyin' is winter," Boffin said.

Dandelion cried, "Merlinda'll be back next spring!"

Kanpur said softly, "What a clever way of describing it, Boffin! But Merlinda will not return to us."

"Will she return as A Person?" Calico Cat asked.

"Oh, no, I couldn't live in the oak tree then," Amelia Airheart groaned.

"Think of having to put clothes on every day!" Calico Cat exclaimed. "There are so many pieces!"

"And they fit so badly!" Dandelion added.

"Merlinda said cleanliness is next to bein' god," Boffin said. "I don't know how bein' god's suppose to feel, but I sort of felt like one around her." Boffin gazed at the woods as though he expected Merlinda to come padding down the path. "She made me feel good inside."

Calico Cat sighed. "When I went to Find It Here, Merlinda's voice kept echoing - 'For those who care about ancestors, that is the sort of thing they care about.' I know who I am without them, she taught me that."

The sky had deepened to purple. Ten Lives rose and padded off slowly. His gruff voice floated through the darkness, "That cushion will never be mine. I didn't know what Merlinda was trying to say when she gave it to me."

The moon rose over the trees and climbed higher and higher until it travelled among the stars, a bright ball in the speckled sky. "It's so beautiful, maybe that's where Merlinda's gone," Dandelion said dreamily.

"I think Merlinda's tellin' me she's glad to see me so happy," Boffin whispered. "Cal'co Cat, I..."

"Look at Dandelion's halo!" Marmeduke interrupted. The moonlight had traced her head in silver.

"Can you see it, Merlinda?" Dandelion purred softly.

Kanpur narrowed her eyes. "I see it also, but I would call it an aura."

Calico Cat sat up. "If those speckled cats and spotty flowered things in *Find It Here* were really cats, Boffin, then that must be a calico cat up there in the sky, maybe the first one ever with the bright eye and many glittering spots and dark splotches, like mine!" Her eyes shone. "That's my ancestor!"

"Ancestors are old," Kanpur said, "old as the stars."

Boffin whispered, "What beautiful ancestors!"

Chapter Fourteen

Spring had arrived; the days were turning mild. Dandelion was lying on the roof of The Room because, she said, she was closer to the sun there. One day she called down, "Here comes Boffin with someone!"

"Another alley cat?" Marmeduke howled.

"Oh please not like the one that followed him home," Calico Cat groaned.

"Or a squirrel," Amelia Airheart muttered, looking behind her. "We have more than enough of them already."

"I hope it eats more neatly than Boffin," Dandelion said. "The food he used to get on his cheeks - yuk!"

Marmeduke glared at the gate. "With Merlinda gone, we are still too many. Of course I wish she were still here, but do we need yet one more stray?"

Boffin jumped over the gate, followed by the stray. Marmeduke scowled while Calico Cat's black whiskers twitched on one cheek, and her white whiskers twitched on the other. Dandelion leapt to the ground and sat so the light sifted through her tufted ears to form a halo. Kanpur was stretched out in her aristocratic pose, one arm flung forward, her head tilted slightly back, her eyes half closed. Marmeduke stirred up a dust storm swishing his tail, prompting Dandelion and Kanpur to sneeze. Above the dust storm, two yellow eyes stared down through the bare branches.

"A garish suit," Marmeduke sniffed.

"Black and white," Kanpur observed.

"Neither black nor white," Calico Cat noted.

"Dapply," Dandelion said, "like a dappled horse."

"Horses aren't dappled," Calico Cat disagreed. "They can be piebald."

"No, it ain't bald," Ten Lives deep voice rumbled. He'd just opened his eyes. "It's rather hairy."

"Longish fur, like yours, Dandelion," Marmeduke said.

"Not quite as long as mine," Dandelion sniffed, licking her side.

"It looks like the ground when the sun shines through the leaves," Amelia Airheart muttered. "When there are leaves." She hated being exposed.

"That's what I said, dapply," Dandelion retorted.

"It would have a suit like mine if it had three colors," Calico Cat noted, adding to herself, "which of course it doesn't have."

"Where'd you find it?" Dandelion asked Boffin as he padded up.

Boffin sat down, yawned, scratched his ear, licked his side, and replied, "The Woman was playin' tennis. It chased a ball that went rollin' down the street."

Marmeduke's eyes widened. "Is The Woman here? My stomach's howling for the treat she promised."

"Nope. She went in one direction and I went in the other and the stray-ger followed me here."

"Its eyes are blue!" Dandelion cried. "Weird!"

"No," Marmeduke said, "that Siamese at the Catsel had blue eyes. They're quite common among Siamese." He'd known only one Siamese, but the others didn't know that.

Kanpur leaned forward. "It's eyes are brown."

Marmeduke sneered, "Cats don't have brown eyes."

Kanpur stared. "There is one brown eye and one blue eye!" The cat eyed Kanpur.

Calico Cat rose. "Really? It must be one of those glass eyes that Persons have." She stuck her nose in the stranger's face. The cat leapt back. "A real brown eye! I wouldn't have believed it if I hadn't seen it myself."

"Does it have a name?" Ten Lives demanded. "Or is she 'cat' like Dandelion was before she woke up?"

"The Woman called it 'Martina' because she chased the tennis ball," Boffin yawned. "The Woman picked her up and figured she's starved. Then she started laughin' at her toes because the fur's stickin' out in every direction, so she added Pop Corn Toes."

"Martina Pop Corn Toes!" Marmeduke hooted.

"Merlinda would've said, 'Martina Pop Corn Toes, what kind of a name is that?'" Calico Cat mimicked.

Dandelion approached the newcomer with a ball in her mouth and dropped it at her feet. "Martina Pop Corn Toes, do you like to play hockey?"

Martina Pop Corn Toes' eyes moved from Dandelion's silver nose to the tip of her plumed tail. Turning to Ten Lives, she asked, "Are you, by any chance, Methuselah?"

"She's a bit forward," Ten Lives muttered to Boffin, "but Merlinda wouldn't have worried about that." Martina Pop Corn Toes looked puzzled. "Merlinda died several months ago, but I can still hear her voice."

"Merlinda. She must have been very special to you."

Everyone shouted, "She was special to all of us!"

Martina Pop Corn Toes brushed each of them with her eyes before she turned back to Ten Lives. "You miss her."

Ten Lives folded his paws. He whispered to Boffin, "She's elegant like Merlinda. I'll tell her my story to make her welcome..." The elder turned to Martina Pop Corn Toes. "Would you like to hear about my lives?"

The clan drifted to distant parts of the yard. Boffin stretched his toes, rose, and slipped away too. He, like they, knew that Ten Lives would begin with his first life, which would lead to the second, the third, and then to all the others right up to the present day. Martina Pop Corn Toes would know all of them well, including Merlinda, especially Merlinda, by the time Ten Lives reached the end. And perhaps, Boffin mused, Martina Pop Corn Toes would become his special friend. Or maybe Calico Cat. Or perhaps Dandelion. Or maybe...